First edition published January 2010

Oftwominds.com
P.O. Box 4727
Berkeley, California 94704

www.oftwominds.com

Survival+: The Primer

An Introduction to Survival+: Structuring Prosperity for Yourself and the Nation

Charles Hugh Smith

Table of Contents

Introduction

With crisis comes opportunity for positive transformation: this is the central theme of *Survival+: Structuring Prosperity for Yourself and the Nation* which I published in October 2009.

Survival+: The Primer is an introduction to many of the key concepts of the full 140,000-word book. While it is impossible to distill all the ideas into a short primer, we can at least address these key understandings:

- The status quo of a rapidly expanding Savior State in thrall to global cartels is heading for inevitable insolvency
- Though the devolution and insolvency of the debt-based status quo is driven by large-scale forces, the opportunities will be small-scale and open to individuals, families and communities.
- Though the forces at work are global, we are not powerless. As individuals, we have the power to create our own transformation.

This can be expressed very simply: we are what we do every day.

In a very real way, we "vote" for our health by what we choose to put in our mouths three times a day, just as we "vote" on which kinds of food and companies we support when we buy the food.

Every purchase we make is a "vote" for or against a high-cost, debt-serf lifestyle that serves the interests of Power Elites and cartels.

Every hour we spend "consuming" mass-media "entertainment" is a "vote" in favor of passivity, powerlessness and propaganda. Every time we turn off the mass media we are "voting" for our own productivity and well-being.

Every time we offer our effort to others in voluntary social networks, we "vote" for the reciprocity and trust which are the foundations of sustainable communities.

Every vote for the incumbent politician is a vote for a doomed status quo that is in servitude to Power Elites (with rare exceptions).

Readers of my weblog often ask for a "checklist" of specific recommendations: jobs to seek, the best locales to move to, etc. But no checklist can apply to us all; we're each a unique mix of interests, talents, history and family/social networks. The only person who can sort out what's best for you is you.

What I can offer is a set of "first principles" which can help guide our analysis and decisionmaking in the Great Transformation ahead.

Chapter One: An Overview

A great clash between what we are told is unfolding and what is actually unfolding lies just ahead.

The status quo "Powers That Be" and its mainstream media repeatedly insist that:

- We have cheap, abundant energy for a long time to come; shortages or permanently costly energy is decades away. We have plenty of time for technological wonders to arise and replace petroleum.
- The Social Security and Medicare entitlements promised to all, though totaling some $50 trillion in excess of projected tax revenues, will be paid; all that is needed are modest policy adjustments.
- The current global financial meltdown was unexpected and could not have been foreseen; it is a temporary "bad patch" which has already been fixed by government intervention and regulatory adjustments.
- Public and private debt can continue expanding three times faster than GDP indefinitely; rising credit and debt are the essential lifeblood of permanent growth.
- Environmental issues such as the stripping of the world's fisheries, dead zones in the Chesapeake Bay, dwindling fresh water aquifers, etc. can all be fixed with modest policy adjustments.
- The consumerist culture that has evolved over the past 60 years is the natural perfection of capitalism, prosperity and American values; Americans are the happiest, most prosperous people on the planet.
- The fast-growing epidemic of obesity and related chronic diseases in the U.S. ("diabesity") is worrisome, but we have the finest healthcare system in the world.

Yet all of the above is demonstrably false.

In reality, the decline of cheap, abundant oil (oil under pressure in supergiant fields) has already begun. The iron laws of demographics dictate the promised entitlements cannot be paid and that Medicare is only a few years away from insolvency. The financial meltdown was not only easily predictable, it was inevitable, as the consequences of systemic fraud, deception, embezzlement, collusion and exponential expansions of risk, debt and leverage could not be held off forever.

The reduction of American culture and values to a one-dimensional "consumerism is the highest good" was not natural, and rather than produce the perfection of capitalism, it has produced the perfection of predatory crony capitalism and an ever-expanding State beholden to a Power Elite which owns or controls the vast majority of the productive assets, wealth, income and lawmaking machinery of the U.S.

Rather than being the happiest people on the planet, Americans are visibly unhappy, anxious, angry, depressed, distracted and all too often heavily sedated with powerful psychotropic medications.

We should wonder if the overzealous dispensation of such drugs masks cultural rather than psychiatric disorders, and an unspoken desire to "treat" these disorders in a relatively low-cost fashion by numbing the patients' awareness of their own alienation, anxiety and unhappiness.

Rather than having the finest healthcare system in the world, we have the most perniciously incentivized system in the industrialized world, a system which consumes a staggering 16% of the nation's entire output but which provides little to no healthcare for tens of millions of citizens and which supplies incredibly costly but largely ineffective care to the elderly covered by an increasingly unaffordable Medicare.

Up to 40% of the entire sum spent on healthcare is paper shuffling, fraud and useless or even harmful "care." Despite this vast outpouring of the nation's wealth, the health of its citizenry continues to decline in measurable ways; this vast expenditure has done nothing to stop the astonishing rise in obesity and related chronic diseases, arguably the most pressing public health issue facing the nation.

In effect, the U.S. healthcare system is bankrupting the nation even as it fails to improve the health of the citizenry at large. It is thus a stupendous failure, creating ever-smaller marginal gains with ever-greater expenditures for questionable tests, drugs and treatments.

Rather than look to an increasingly unhealthy diet and lifestyle, the "sick-care" system seeks ever more costly "treatments" and pharmaceutical "fixes" for complex chronic diseases which are simply not curable by "magic bullet" drugs.

Contrary to the constantly repeated assurances of The Powers That Be, modest policy modifications are not replenishing the nation's fisheries or ground water, nor is tweaking the parameters of various systems reversing environmental and economic decline.

You may think these assessments are sensationalist, harsh or even offensive. That is not my intention. I believe the evidence is overwhelming that all these soothing contentions pressed upon us by the Powers That Be on a daily basis are in fact false.

If this assertion is true, the vast majority of what is "reported" and "consumed" as "news" is essentially propaganda, either conscious or subconscious.

If the status quo's intellectual justification for their dominance is fundamentally false, then we can anticipate the wholesale destruction of that justification as events undermine all the self-serving propaganda.

As a result, we will have to construct an alternative understanding of our world which aligns far more closely to reality than the current status quo's complacent faith in a decaying, failing system.

If this is true, then we have no time left for distracting debates about policy tweaks and hairsplitting; the time such modifications could have any measurable impact are long gone. We have run out of time for trivializing conversations along ginned-up ideological lines, "I'm a conservative and you're a liberal" and the mass media's entertainment-passed-off-as-analysis. We have also run out of time for the easy distractions of complexity itself, the unspoken idea that things are now too complex to modify in any meaningful way.

Reality, in contrast, has no problem adjusting complexity downward.

If all the fundamental contentions of the Powers That Be are demonstrably false, we are forced to ask why they press them so persuasively on us.

The answer to this critical question can be found by asking *cui bono*: to whose benefit? Although we are constantly told the system benefits all of us, that it is the very perfection of prosperity, free market capitalism and thus of happiness itself, this is also demonstrably false.

This leads to the conclusion that the entire intellectual structure which supports and enables the U.S. economy, government and culture is nonsense, and those pushing it so mightily and perseverently are doing so out of a highly refined self-interest--a self-interest which does not magically better the nation or those not fortunate enough to belong to the Elite (the Plutocracy) or to its *high-caste* technocratic workforce.

These are troubling assertions, and they require careful analysis.

Before you decide this is merely sensationalist, please read the following analysis and look into the sourced books. Compare your own lived experience and intuitions with the mass media's "happy story" that everything is just fine, minor financial perturbations have been resolved and a consumerist Utopia is still firmly in place.

It is my contention that the global meltdown has exposed the

Plutocracy's *over-reach* via ever-larger bets, ever-riskier leverage and ever-larger redistributions of national income to its own coffers. To protect its interests and dominance, it must defend at all costs the intellectual framework that enables its dominance.

Thus there is a whiff of desperation in its campaign to convince the world that this is not at heart a global crisis which threatens to bring down the entire structure but a "normal" if slightly deeper recession which has already been repaired by the usual "fix" of State manipulation of interest rates and money supply.

We must be alert to the concentrated ownership/control of the mass media, and to the overwhelming need of the global Elites to reassure their restive, anxious populaces that the structure of Elite dominance and wealth is robust, secure, and in the populace's self-interest.

We must also be alert to the irony that the Elite's first task is to convince the underclasses that there is no Elite, no Powers That Be and no Plutocracy. While there is no "membership" card in the Plutocracy, the simple facts of concentrated ownership, influence and income roughly define that class. Conflicts between various segments of the Elite does not mean there is no Plutocracy--it only means that greed and over-reach naturally set up some shuffling and pushing to head the line.

In actuality, the structure is not in the populace's self interest, and it is increasingly insecure, brittle, and vulnerable to decay and/or disruption on numerous levels. Much of the vulnerability stems not from Elite over-reach but from the fact that we as a species have reached the carrying capacity of the planet in terms of a high-energy consumption dependency on cheap abundant petroleum for food, transport, water, "growth," etc.

Nonetheless those who control the vast majority of assets, wealth, and tools of persuasion have the most to gain from a continuing belief in the system's stability. Thus their defense of the system which serves their interests above all else will be fierce and unremitting.

The Plutocracy is not a conspiracy in the formal sense of a membership which gathers like the Bohemian Club or even an informal assemblage such as the Bilderberg Group. "Membership" is granted solely by great wealth and control of productive assets; political influence flows from that.

People who control, say, $100 million or more (via family ownership or managerial position) tend to meet one another socially or to do business, and while they jockey for advantage within a group like the rest of us, they form a small class of citizens possessing virtually unimpaired political influence.

Thus in describing a Plutocracy I am not positing a conspiracy but simply a financial elite which controls some 2/3 of the productive wealth of the U.S. This is simply a statement of fact. Their collective self-interest is in maintaining the conceptual, legal and financial systems which enable their continued dominance of wealth and influence.

People with similar self-interests naturally band together in *self-organizing networks* and groups to protect those interests, and since information is power then the inner workings of various *self-organizing groups* are confidential as part of that self-protection.

Thus when I speak of The Plutocracy I refer not to a formal conspiracy with meetings and officers but to a self-organized Elite based on protecting their ownership of 2/3 of the productive wealth of the nation. As each acts to protect his/her wealth at the highest reaches of influence (tax shelters, tax breaks, legislative exclusions, legal rulings, etc.) then they are also acting to defend their class.

The notion that a rentier-financial Elite wields largely hidden sway over much of the U.S. wealth, political process and media is not new.

Indeed, the evidence describing this Elite is widely available in books such as: How The World Really Works, The Rich and the Super-Rich (out of print, but used copies are available), Tragedy & Hope: A History of the World in Our Time, Wealth and Democracy: A Political History of the American Rich, The Power Elite and This Land Is Their Land: Reports from a Divided Nation.

What I term the Plutocracy has been fully documented. To question its existence and power is not a matter of opinion but of misinformation.

Why would intelligent middle-class people support a conceptual system that so heavily favors an Elite over the common good? Certainly self-interest plays a major role. If you are reporting events and trends that undermine your employers' wealth and power, you may well conclude that favoring the status quo in all matters will protect your career, income and status far more effectively than announcing the Emperor has no clothes.

In some cases, otherwise independent-minded people have never encountered a serious critique of the status quo's conceptual foundation and thus they believe that understanding of the world is "obvious."

Without a skeptical accounting of *cui bono* (to whose benefit?) then what is "obvious" will naturally tend to defend and support a status quo which has labored to construct and defend an "obviousness" which protects its own wealth, ownership and influence.

As its own interests diverge from those of society at large, the Plutocracy has an irresistible incentive to foster the illusion that policies which benefit the Elites also benefit the middle class. As the Plutocracy and its mass media minions trumpet the benefits of the free market, these same Elites work with unremitting zeal to exempt themselves and their State factotums from these very same free market forces.

Lastly, the status quo understanding of the world is that any problem is inherently "fixable" with minor policy adjustments. Thus even as the global financial pyramid of highly leveraged debts unravels, the status quo response is bureaucratic shuffling of oversight duties, minor tweaking of regulatory rules trumpeted as "major fixes" and behind the scenes, trillion-dollar bailouts of the Plutocracy funded by taxpayers.

When the non-Elite citizen comes to understand this, a new mechanism takes hold that I call *when belief in the system fades*.

This is how empires fall: complacency joins hands with self-aggrandizement.

There are four other subtle processes at work in the erosion of the system's intellectual foundation:

1. Elites and underclass alike respond to the visible crumbling of the empire with a sublime complacency grounded in vague appeals to some mythical past spirit which will magically arise to enthuse a torpid, self-absorbed Elite and populace. In the U.S., appeals are made to "the can-do spirit" which powered America's past confidence and resolve.

Unfortunately for both the Elite and the underclass (both of whom depend on State largesse and a vibrant middle class paying high taxes), rousing but ultimately empty incantations are no substitute for difficult choices, tradeoffs and sacrifices.

2. Even as interconnected crises afflict the empire, the Elite moves deeper into a self-aggrandizement marked by pervasive over-reach. Having mastered its influence over the State, the Plutocracy finds few limits or obstacles to its over-reach.

This over-reach has the characteristics of a positive feedback loop: the more wealth the Elite controls, the greater its influence, which then enables even more wealth acquisition, and so on.

3. As a result, the interests of the Plutocracy and thus the State diverge from the common interests of the citizenry as a whole. This widening structural imbalance of power creates cynicism and a *profound political disunity* that cripples any attempt at structural solutions.

Given that any real solution would reduce the Plutocracy and State's share of the national income, both will resist all structural change, preferring stagnation to any reduction in their income and power.

One of the single most powerful mechanisms at play is *windfall exploitation*.

Windfalls in Nature are rare, and thus all organisms are selected to exploit them as fully as possible--gorging, so to speak, on any newfound riches. The Plutocracy's influence enables it to suppress or weaken counterforces (such as regulatory systems) and thus open up windfalls which it can then exploit.

For example: having dispensed with troublesome barriers between finance and banking and nettlesome limitations on securities ratings and off-balance sheet assets, investment bankers opened up new windfalls: mortgage-backed securities, bogus "low-risk" ratings, CDOs and other derivatives, and so on.

A second related mechanism is *over-reach*.

As barriers to Plutocratic expansion topple and the Elites' share of national income rises, then a positive feedback loop forms: the more the Plutocracy expands, the greater the profits, which then fuels greater political influence, and so on. At a critical (and largely invisible) juncture the Plutocracy inevitably over-reaches.

Over-reach takes many forms. It might be an unparalleled expansion into highly risky derivatives, or a domestic Plutocracy reaching into international speculations. The key point is that over-reach pushes the Elites' financial speculations beyond a level of known, controllable risk into uncharted territory, a territory which promises stupendous profits along with equally stupendous but obscured risk.

Over-reach inevitably pushes a stable system into instability.

Once the Plutocracy's income, power and influence are threatened by the rising instability caused by over-reach, then the Elite resorts to propaganda and other mechanisms to mask the structural instability from the populace. The hope is that the system which so greatly benefits the Plutocracy can be restored to health, but the mechanisms of "recovery" are essentially inauthentic: *simulacra* of reform, propagandistic manipulations of economic data to mask the structural instability, and outright looting of State resources (bailouts, etc.)--that is, publicly-funded exemptions from free market forces that would otherwise require the Plutocracy to absorb the consequences of its leveraged gambles.

This failure to address the underlying causes--systemic over-reach and Plutocratic domination of the economy and political system--insures the instability will only worsen. As ever-more frantic attempts to protect the interests of the Plutocracy fail, then another feedback loop forms: the more sham reforms and State bailouts fail to restore stability, the more desperate the Plutocracy's attempts to retain power.

It is worth recalling that the average compensation for the 10 top hedge fund managers during the go-go years of the 2000s was $600 million each. That is not a typo. This is an excellent (if extreme) example of over-reach and windfall exploitation.

As it enriches itself via semi-legal or simply officially sanctioned looting, fraud, deception, embezzlement, collusion, "sweetheart" State contracts, tax avoidance, environmental loopholes and a hundred other mechanisms of over-reach and windfall exploitation, the Elite inadvertently provides the lower classes with a compelling example of increasing wealth via fraud and manipulation rather than production.

Both the *high-caste* technocrats (who keep the State and economy running smoothly for their Plutocratic overlords) and the underclass sense their shares of the national income and wealth are diminishing as the Plutocracy diverts a greater share to their own pockets; quite naturally they seek some way to maintain or grow their own declining purchasing power/wealth.

As they watch the Plutocrats in action, they learn the most effective ways to increase one's share of the income/wealth are looting ("gaming the system" of pensions, benefits, State entitlements, etc.), deception, fraud and embezzlement (accounting trickery, collusion, sweetheart contracts, etc.) and influence-peddling, known in the Third World as corruption, baksheesh, etc.

As the middle class increasingly runs afoul of the byzantine, Kafkaesque regulations imposed by an ever-expanding State, they find that financial leverage and legerdemain is far more lucrative than actually producing goods and services.

Unsurprisingly, the Plutocracy finds ways to gain exemptions, loopholes and special dispensations that greatly reduce the reach of regulations and taxes that burden middle class entrepreneurs.

As the middle class abandons thrift and production for financial speculation and highly leveraged debt (following the example of their Plutocratic overlords), tax revenues soar as leveraged speculation pyramids into bubbles, enabling vast expansions of a State which is inherently seeking constant expansion of its income and powers.

When these financial bubbles eventually deflate, then tax revenues plummet as productive work and investment have declined. Why bother working hard when the big, easy money is made via leveraged speculation? Only fools would tolerate all the regulatory costs and high taxes imposed on producing goods and services; far easier to speculate in bubbling assets like housing, stocks, energy, etc.

The State responds to this drop in tax revenues by raising taxes on the remaining productive middle class, creating a positive feedback loop which reinforces the incentives to either drop out, move to speculation or game the system.

Though heavily marginalized, the underclass also copies the Plutocrats' lead by gaming whatever entitlements the State offers to buy the underclasses' silence, passivity and compliance. Thus petty corruption and fraud increases in all State entitlement programs as every sector of society seeks to suck off the maximum benefits while contributing the least possible to the public coffers.

Thus does a nation built on the sacrifices and communal spirit of its citizenry degrade into a doomed culture of self-aggrandizement in which sacrifice is for suckers and looting, manipulation, fraud, embezzlement, debauchery of credit, leverage and the pursuit of speculative riches are the order of the day from the Plutocracy on down through the technocratic upper caste to the underclass.

4. In a society with what we might term an *adult understanding* of the world, it is understood that difficult trade-offs are a necessary part of life. One cannot pursue every path at once, acquire every desired object at once or learn every skill at once. Priorities must be established via vigorous, open-minded debate (either within oneself for one's own decisions or within the nation-State for larger issues) and a painful triage laid down in which some wants are set aside in favor of actual needs.

Broadly speaking, this is the result of a cost-benefit analysis. Items with increasingly higher marginal costs and increasingly lower marginal returns (a topic covered later) are sacrificed in favor of projects with low costs and high returns. This is, after all, mere common sense.

This painful "adult" process has been replaced in the U.S. by a *permanent adolescence* in which accountability, integrity and trade-offs have been banished by stupendous borrowing. Infantile tantrums and various states of psychological denial have crowded out open-minded discussion; every want has been funded by breathtakingly massive borrowing by the State, private enterprise and households alike.

Once the thick shield of denial is finally pierced by events, it is replaced by the search for an external force or agency to blame for self-destructive indulgences. Personal responsibility, integrity and accountability are set aside in favor of an adolescent sputtering rage.

A pernicious, largely unexamined legal system creates tremendous incentives for unnecessary actions designed to ward off lawsuits, feeding vast armies of high-caste technocratic parasites who produce nothing in the way of wealth-producing goods and services even as they burden the remaining productive sector with make-work rules and costly strategies to avoid potentially ruinous lawsuits.

In true Orwellian fashion, much of this parasitism is described by its practitioners as protecting the "little guy" from the oppressive Elite and State. But as the Plutocracy and State increase their share of the national wealth at the expense of the citizenry, this claim rings increasingly hollow.

Thus we have seniors covered by Medicare receiving multiple costly (and often useless) tests designed less to identify the active causes of disease than to shield the practitioners from lawsuits and to enrich those administering the tests.

Meanwhile, millions of non-elderly citizens cannot obtain even a single test as they lack the benefits provided to State and corporate elites.

Rather than face the impossibility of funding such a fiscally bankrupt system of parasitism and profiteering, we as a nation have simply borrowed trillions of dollars to stave off any painful prioritizing.

Very few weapons systems are ever cancelled for the same reasons; the profiteering by a few enterprises and the contributions they make to lawmakers insure that every weapons system will receive funding, even if that requires borrowing gargantuan sums year after year.

This evasion of hard choices (and free market forces) via endlessly rising debt will eventually bring down the nation's currency and its debt-ridden State. The irony is that this carefree self-indulgent adolescent avoidance of cost-benefit analysis guarantees systemic collapse.

Let's begin our search for an *integrated understanding* with a look at how over-reach, windfall exploitation and the divergence of Elite/State and middle-class interests illuminate the disintegration of post-World War II America into the present Depression.

1. The great postwar income convergence (i.e. the rise of the great middle class, the reduction of poverty and the relative reduction of the Plutocracy's share of national income) reverses in the early 1970s as the "true prosperity" of the postwar era ends and is replaced by income flowing increasingly to the top as stagflation, globalization and the decline of the dollar gut the purchasing power of the middle class.

2. The rising productivity of the 50s and 60s slips to the flatline through the 70s and early 80s, only picking up again as computers revolutionize the back office, sales, manufacturing, just-in-time shipping/production, etc.

3. Concurrent with this gradual return to increasing productivity is the rise of finance as the key profit-center of corporate America. As income skews ever more heavily to the top 1%/5%, then capital (productive assets) become ever more heavily concentrated in the hands of the rentier-financial Plutocracy. The top 1% now owns some 2/3 of the nation's entire productive wealth.

4. As profits rise (from rising productivity) then the profits flow not to wages (which remain flat to down 1975-2009 for all but the top 10% upper-caste professional class) but to those who own the capital.

5. As the middle class experiences a decline in their income and purchasing power (due to the declining dollar, rising income disparity, and wages falling due to global wage arbitrage) then they take on ever-larger debts to fund what they have been brainwashed by the media to believe is "the American dream" of imported luxury goods, expansive homes, overseas cruises, etc.

The only other mechanism available to the middle class to increase household income is for Mom/Aunt/Grandma to enter the workforce, which she does in the tens of millions, with sociological consequences which are still unfolding.

6. This media-driven desire to borrow to fund the "good life" is hugely profitable to the money-center and investment banks, which expand rapidly into mortgage securitization, derivatives and consumer credit to

the point that they come to dominate corporate profits.

7. The financial Plutocracy, observing that producing goods is not very profitable unless you can fix prices or gain government subsidies and tax giveaways (oil lease depreciation, etc.) sinks its capital into the FIRE economy (finance, insurance and real estate), eschewing real-world investments as comparatively unprofitable.

Though rarely noted, this is a longstanding trait of capitalism stretching back to 1400-era Venice. When trade became less profitable than mainland farming, the Venetian Elite stopped funding trade and bought farms on the mainland. As a side effect, Venice ceased to be a military and trading power. But the Elite remained immensely wealthy.

8. As the tech bubble expands, middle-class investors see the Plutocracy (those with enough capital to qualify as angel investors and vulture, oops, I mean venture capitalists) reaping huge gains, and they enter the dot-com stock bubble buildup with a vengeance.

9. In a happy accident, the Soviet Empire collapses just as productivity begins its computer-fueled rise in the U.S. In a so-called Unipolar World in which U.S. military, political and financial influence is unrivaled, non-U.S. investors seek the relative safety and high returns (based on appreciation of the dollar) of U.S. financial instruments.

10. The dot-com bubble implodes in a speculative meltdown, and retail investors (a.k.a. the middle class 401K investors) are devastated. The ephemeral wealth they once possessed, however briefly, fuels their speculative desire to get into the next get-rich-quick game, which just so happens to be "something everyone understands:" real estate.

11. Having exhausted the dot-com play, Plutocratic capital is seeking a new high-profit home. The miracles of derivatives (CDOs, credit default swaps, etc.) and securitized debt (mortgage tranches, etc.) open up vast new opportunities for leverage, off-balance sheet shenanigans and outright fraud. As chip wafer plants disappear from Silicon Valley (too dirty, costly, etc.) then they're replaced with paper: mortgage-backed securities. (Over-reach and windfall exploitation writ large.)

12. Sniffing gold in them thar exurban hills, the under-capitalized and over-indebted U.S. working class and middle class reach for the chalice of easy-money gold: leveraged real estate. (Over-reach and windfall exploitation writ small.)

13. With the Federal financial regulatory agencies in a Republican/Democrat-enforced somnambulance, the coast is clear for

brigands, shysters, fraudsters, con artists, liars, cheats, and assorted riff-raff in the realty, mortgage and appraisal businesses, who all feed the ravenous maw of the money-center banks' apparently limitless appetite for real estate assets to securitize and leverage in exotic and stupendously profitable ways.

14. For a wonderful five years circa 2002-2006, the game is afoot and no-down-payment Jill and $100 million-bonus Jack are immensely enriched. Meanwhile, the underlying real economy is becoming ever more imbalanced and ever more fragile as real production and real productivity plummet as everyone rushes to the speculative riches of exurban McMansions and malls.

15. Elite and middle-class interests seem to converge during this speculative mania: everyone is benefiting from the real estate bubble except the poor, who are bought off with minimal social welfare programs and endless entertainment (via TV) then safely ignored, as they don't vote or spend.

But this convergence was illusory; while the Plutocracy and State functionaries benefited (via stupendous capital gains for the former and vastly richer pension promises for the latter), the private-sector middle class is in essence the bag-holder: when the newfound "wealth" in housing and stock market gains vanish, it is the middle class wealth which is destroyed en masse.

16. This last best speculative leveraged credit bubble pops (alas, exponential expansion of credit cannot go on forever), gutting the stock market which had grown utterly dependent on leverage, debt, gamed/fraudulent accounting and asset bubbles for its rising profits.

17. Doubly devastated by the implosion of housing and their stock investments (mostly in 401K and IRA retirement funds), the middle class faces the terrible consequences of its 26-year stupor of ever-rising debt and leverage. Alas, the Emperor's clothes are revealed as remarkably transparent.

18. Having borrowed and squandered trillions of dollars since 1981 on unaffordable entitlements, military misadventures and assorted bridges-to-nowhere pork spending, the Federal government finds its ability to borrow its way out of its current debt hole annoyingly limited. The rest of the world shuns Treasury debt and works to create an alternative reserve currency, shutting down the "dollar con" (we take your tangible goods and give you paper in return.)

19. With the global media concentrated in a scant few corporate hands (less than 10), this pulling away of the curtain is excised from media coverage in a ruthless campaign of pure propaganda.

20. As the wheels fall off the U.S. economy and the bubbles cannot be re-inflated, fruitless attempts at holding back the tide with incantations (stop, tide, I speak for the U.S. Treasury!) and loopy sand castles (the bottom is in, buy now!) abound. Unresponsive to propaganda, the real world grinds down into a global Depression without visible end.

If we do nothing, we will be swept along in the Great Descent. Alternatively, if we want to prosper, then we must first gain an integrated understanding of all the interlocking crises we face.

Toward an Integrated Understanding

This process of bridging the widening gap between what we experience and what we're told we should be experiencing via the substitution of simulacra for authentic structures is central to this entire analysis.

Why are the State and the Plutocracy (two sides of the same coin) substituting simulacra for authentic structures and truthful accounts? Let's answer by asking: what would a truthful accounting of *cui bono*-- to whose benefit?--reveal?

A truthful accounting would reveal that the status quo benefits the rentier-financial Elite and high-caste technocrats at the expense of the rest of us.

That is, the 99% who do not own 2/3 of the productive assets of the nation and the 75% who do not belong to the State/technocrat upper-caste which serves the system for its own self-aggrandizement.

In sum: a truthful accounting of *cui bono* would result in the exposure of the over-reach, exploitation, deception, fraud, mismanagement, manipulation and self-aggrandizement of the Plutocracy and its high-caste State/corporate technocracy (two "masters," one system). A truthful accounting would result in the shattering of the illusion that supporting the status quo is in your self-interest.

Maintaining this illusion is the key to maintaining the Plutocracy and the State's share of the national income. This explains why the Plutocracy and the State (two sides of one coin) are obsessed with creating sham structures and narratives designed to lull the citizenry into the comforting illusion that they are the beneficiaries of:

- Democracy (when 98% of incumbents win re-election, can that be authentic democracy?)
- Free press (when a handful of corporations own the vast majority of the print/broadcast/radio/web media and the State manipulates statistics without media challenge, can that be an authentic "free press"?)
- Higher education (a factory for producing high-caste overseers /enforcers for the State/Plutocracy Plantation)
- Healthcare (a quarter of the citizenry have no healthcare, another quarter have sham "coverage")
- "Ownership" (of debt and rapidly declining collateral--the perfect setup for debt-serfdom)
- Low-tax (low tax for the Plutocracy and unproductive class, high tax for the dwindling productive class) "free enterprise" (crony Capitalism).

To maintain their share of the dwindling national income, it is essential that the Plutocracy and State mask the devolution and insolvency of the State. The primary prop of non-elite *belief in the system* is the faith that the *Savior State* will fund everyone's retirement, healthcare and security as promised--a promise that cannot be fulfilled. (A *Savior State* promises to save everyone from personal responsibility via entitlements funded by demographic and financial fraud.)

As a result of this pervasive substitution of sham structures and narratives, truth evaporates, replaced by deception and propaganda.

Transparency is replaced by obscurity and staged entertainments are presented as "news" or "democracy in action."

Facts are replaced by massaged statistics; accounting is replaced by trickery. Common purpose is replaced by self-aggrandizement and game-the-system looting.

The Elites' interests diverge from those of the society as a whole, and the result is a *profound political disunity* of hardened, embittered camps warring over the remaining spoils of a decaying State.

Regulations are replaced by protection schemes and layers of purposefully impenetrable obfuscation that exempts the Elites from market forces (risk and subsequent losses).

Healthcare is replaced by a highly profitable facsimile in which 25% of the citizenry receive no care and another 25% pay for sham "healthcare coverage" which offers little to no actual care. The high-caste class of State and corporate technocrats is rewarded for their services to the State/Plutocracy with full coverage. (Observe the parallels to State employees' coveted positions in Third World kleptocracies.)

The free press is replaced with a corporate media tasked with protecting the interests of the State and Plutocracy that owns it lock, stock and barrel.

Truthfulness is replaced by lies, deception, trickery and a pervasive, willful obscurity in every level of society and the economy.

Simulacra of capital are passed off as assets. A sham prosperity based on exponential growth of credit is presented as "capitalism." Misallocation of capital and looting are masked as "market forces."

Incomplete, misleading, and romanticized information is presented as "fact" while truthful accountings are suppressed and undermined.

Lived experience is *derealized* by ever-present media fantasies ("we have the finest healthcare system in the world," "the banking sector is free enterprise at its finest," etc.) and the schizophrenic gap between experience and media fantasy is papered over with drugs (prescribed, illegal and legal) and distractions (celebrity worship, entertainment/ sports, narcissistic indulgences, shopping, etc.)

Dissent is filtered into distracting, meaningless "ideological conflicts" of no substance, "debates" which leave the Power Elite and State in control of the national income.

Obesity, passivity and addiction are incentivized as poor nutrition and chronic illnesses are the highest-return "profit centers" for the agribusiness/packaged/fast-food industry and the "healthcare" (actually sick-care) industry.

The destructive consequences of the status quo are systematically internalized as personal failings: lack of will power, poor judgment, etc.; a simulacrum of "personal responsibility" masks the internalization of master narratives which leave the Plutocracy and State safely unaccountable.

From the perspective of a media sustained by marketing, the ideal internal state is a deep, unresolvable insecurity which can be temporarily soothed by shopping/entertainment.

A simulacrum of citizenship reduces a self-directed populace to passive "consumers."

This process is so subtle and subconscious that it is difficult to discern. But once you understand this substitution mechanism, a type of enlightenment occurs; you no longer accept simulacrum for "the real thing," and the State/Plutocracy has lost your compliance, that is, your belief in the system's fair accounting of your self-interest.

This conflict between direct, lived experience of our ever-worsening problems and the State/Elites' "ignore reality, keep believing in our system" machinery causes a pervasive cultural and individual schizophrenia which causes participants to feel adrift, depressed, alienated, isolated and misunderstood.

The Elites' intellectual framework has a ready response to this ever-widening divide between their increasingly rickety narrative and reality: the metaphors of illness and medicine. Thus the "solution" to the deep misgivings of those who sense the divide between a false narrative and their own experience is prescription medications in quantity.

This growing gulf between lived experience and the Elites' heavily hyped narrative of how our world works eventually causes an enlightenment in some of the managerial/technocrat caste: their belief in the system fades and they drop out.

Once they realize the institutions they have given their lives to will fail, they either withdraw or begin work on an alternative framework of understanding based on their own experience. In seeking experience-based ways to understand our challenges and potential solutions which don't simply serve and enrich Elites, they become part of The Remnant, a self-selected assembly of citizenry who lead by example, not exhortation--in other words, the advance guard of a sustainable economy and free society.

The Remnant is a diverse and self-organizing group of people who are skeptical of overly simplistic contexts and solutions, and skeptical of the Elites' authority structures (the prison/drug gulag, taxation of everything and everyone but the sheltered Elites, recruitment of the poor to military service so the Elites' offspring need not serve, a food and "healthcare" system which encourages illness and chronic ill-health as the most profitable possible conditions, etc.)

The Remnant has learned that the Power Elite has essentially rendered itself unaccountable and thus the consequences of its vast over-reach will fall not on its own small membership but the ill-prepared citizenry below.

The entrenched high-caste technocrats are busy looting the coffers of the State on behalf of themselves and their Plutocrat Masters, and this large caste will only wither when the State becomes insolvent--the end-game of the current borrow-and-spend debt orgy which has sustained the American economy, Plutocracy and State for decades.

Thus the Remnant is preparing for life without State largesse, because the State will no longer be able to borrow or print enough money to support its increasingly burdensome castes, entitlements and fiefdoms. In my terminology, the Remnant's goal is radical self-reliance.

Lastly, The Remnant is acutely aware that the environmental, financial and FEW (food, energy, water) dilemmas facing the planet are not ones of interpretation; they are very real and cannot be explained away or "framed" out of existence with appeals to soothingly vague future technocratic wonders.

This book is an attempt to strip away the obfuscatory intellectual framework which has cloaked and protected the Elites' self-serving over-reach. It is an attempt to speak directly to the real problems we face. Once we understand our own experience and the world directly then the messy realities of various solutions and trade-offs will become clearer.

Then we will have to choose which trade-offs have the best chances for long-term success. The goal is to construct a sustainable, productive economy and a political culture based not on self-serving game-the-system looting but on *the radical self-reliant* appreciation of the fundamental rights to life, liberty and the pursuit of happiness.

End note: I know this must strike some readers as lunacy; the State cannot possibly dissolve in insolvency. Others will be tempted to enter the merry-go-round "debate" as to whether the State should or should not be a "Savior." It doesn't matter; the State cannot print up $100 trillion without reducing the value of the dollar to zero, nor can it fund the military/finance Empire, its own domestic fiefdoms and the Savior State entitlements now promised to 300 million citizens without borrowing/printing $100 trillion. So however you care to calculate the end-state, it remains the same: the devolution and insolvency of the Empire/Savior State.

Chapter Two: The Crisis of Predatory Global Capitalism

It is both tempting and instructive to compare the current crisis of global capitalism with past crises such as the Great Depression of the 1930s or the long period of turmoil from 1873 to 1894.

To the degree the current crisis is financial, then seeking echoes in past crises makes perfect sense. But to the degree we also face unprecedented energy and environmental crises, then these past periods of financial distress cannot be accurate models.

Several other factors make the current global crisis unique. Globalization has expanded to an unprecedented degree, and governments have responded to the collapse of credit by transferring unimaginable levels of risky debt onto the backs of taxpayers, all in the vain hope of reviving a model of "permanent growth" which has run its course: the *Neoliberal* iteration of advanced capitalism which depends on stupendous credit expansion, government intervention to ward off implosion, and on an ever-expanding global predation of markets.

We should also be mindful that the level of deception, obfuscation, fraud, securitization, misrepresentation and State collusion with private looting, and excessive systemic risk-taking are beyond the reach of any previous private speculative frenzies. With truth debased, public faith in a self-serving State-Plutocracy will collapse along with predatory capitalism's promise of permanent prosperity.

This implosion of public trust might well find an echo or analog in the great transformations of the 1960s and early 1970s, when faith in the economy and State foundered under a barrage of government lies and economic decline.

As the state and its Plutocracy fail to reinflate the speculative credit-based asset bubbles which fueled advanced capitalism's last decade of bogus "prosperity," their relentless campaign to convince their citizenry that the system is sound and beneficial to all will be revealed as illusion. At that point values may suddenly shift and old loyalties and beliefs in the system will be jettisoned in favor of more sustainable value systems.

Globalization: Neoliberal Capitalism's Last "Fix"

In essence, globalization was Neoliberal Capitalism's attempt to save itself from the endgame of advanced capitalism foreseen by Marx:

overcapacity which leads to a collapse in profits and thus a decline in capital and the overall economy.

Marx's insight was straightforward: the dynamic of capitalism is for production to rise to meet demand--and then keep rising. As demand is sated, capacity continues to grow because Capital is like a shark--it must move forward or it dies, and it moves toward what was immensely profitable in the recent past.

This is how we get overbuilding of office and retail space: as demand (and profits) soar, then everyone with capital rushes in to enjoy the profit spree. But ironically, this massive rush to the most profitable return guarantees overbuilding and overcapacity.

As Marx noted, supply soon overshoots demand and sales plummet, wiping out profits. The end result is a move to monopoly capital, in which a handful of the strongest players squeeze out or buy out all the weaker players who fold as the return on capital goes negative (losses). The last players standing then consolidate and shutter most of the capacity, setting up a monopoly which then lowers supply below demand to maintain outsized profits.

All the workers laid off as capacity is shuttered no longer have income so they stop spending, which lowers demand even further. This cycle of boom and bust was inherent to Capitalism and Marx expected them to steadily become ever more extreme.

But capitalism "solved" this cycle of overcapacity and crashing demand/income/profits by turning to new overseas markets. Those with a military-backed Empire (for instance, Great Britain) could simply force new markets for domestic goods into existence overseas: by requiring consumers in India to buy British cloth, for instance.

In other cases, advanced capitalist states opened new markets by forcing less developed economies to "offer" their low-cost manufactured goods, which quickly took market share from the more informally produced local goods.

The heyday of colonialism was driven by a simple "virtuous cycle" (virtuous for the advanced economy, not for the subjugated colony) in which the colony was forced to ship its raw materials to the colonial power at low cost while at the same time it was forced to pay a premium for the advanced economy's output/surplus goods.

Since the colonial power's domestic workforce benefited immensely from this "global trade" (low commodity prices thanks to the exploited colonies and plentiful jobs to make the goods forced onto the colonies) then the Colonial Power's Elites received great political support for the their one-sided "globalization" policies.

Apologists are quick to point out the supposedly stupendous benefits of this globalization for the "natives": high-quality advanced goods and paying work in an economy with little formal employment. Yet the reality is not so happy-happy: only economies with locally owned productive capacity such as Japan and Korea become wealthy economies. Those former colonies where foreign capital dominates the productive capacity and commodity extraction are in essence still exploited colonies.

Government ownership is also no panacea.

When less-developed economies' primary assets (including commodities like oil) are owned and operated by the government, then the nation actually becomes poorer, not wealthier, due to the perverse dynamic of the State (government) and capital.

As profits roll in, the State, unlike private capital, defers investment in favor of political patronage and the spoils of "leadership." The incentives to politicians and the State's technocrat managers is thus to eat their seed corn whenever possible, where private capital understands that surplus capital must be invested or deployed in search of high returns lest it dwindle to zero as all profits are extracted and spent.

This mechanism is called the *paradox of plenty* in which resource-rich nations such as Venezuela and Argentina grow progressively more impoverished under State control of the nation's assets.

A corollary of this mechanism is the impoverishment of oil-exporting nations who find redistributing the wealth created by fossil fuels much easier than creating a productive labor force and infrastructure. Thus as the income from oil gyrates (and as oil inevitably enters the depletion phase) then the nation has no cultural or economic Plan B to generate national income and wealth.

With these mechanisms in mind, we can see that the advanced economies attempted to save Capitalism by colonizing China for production and their own domestic populations for credit-based consumption.

Of the many misconceptions about China's spectacular economic growth, perhaps none is more misleading than the assumption that the capital and surplus profits being made in China will stay in China. Despite the much-touted public ownership of joint-venture companies, much of the profitable production in China is owned by non-PRC (People's Republic of China) companies based in Taiwan, Japan, Korea and the West.

From a more clear-eyed perspective, China has been colonized by advanced economies to lower the cost of production and to establish a dumping ground for environmentally unsound production that their domestic citizenry will no longer tolerate. As with all colonies, the profits are extracted and sent elsewhere while apologists are hired to tout the glories of employment for China's millions.

Until, of course, Marx's overcapacity cycle kicks in.

Now that China's stupendous production capacity exceeds the potential demand of the entire world, including its own mostly impoverished domestic populace, then capital is fleeing China in its usual pursuit of higher returns, leaving behind tens of millions of unemployed workers and a toxic landscape.

The Chinese State is now attempting to counter this cycle by spending its own capital on stimulus, but State spending is not a replacement for capital or organic demand. Even worse, the Chinese State saddled its own banks with hundreds of billions of dollars in uncollectible debt in a vain attempt to prop up thousands of State-owned enterprises which racked up gigantic losses even during the boom.

The Chinese State attempted to staunch this open wound by closing thousands of its factories but the uncollectible debts remain, buried by accounting tricks within the books of its four major banks and government finance ministries.

The bloom is off the rose now that the overcapacity in China is no longer profitable to global capital and in essence the Chinese State is left holding the bag: stupendous losses in its own financial system, horrendously costly environmental damage and an industrial infrastructure which is losing value as capital shifts elsewhere.

Meanwhile, advanced Capitalism expanded due to two key innovations: the colonization of its own domestic consumers and the exponential increase in speculative debt instruments.

The essence of colonization is the forcing opening of new markets for surplus production. Frustrated by the poverty of 80% of the Chinese and Indian populaces--people with almost no surplus income cannot consume much in the way of surplus production--global capitalism turned to its own domestic populaces.

By lowering the cost of money to near-zero and generating a gigantic asset bubble in the one asset every middle class consumer already owned--a house--then global capital in essence colonized its own domestic populaces by opening a heretofore limited market for surplus production: a consumerist blow-off of unprecedented scope fueled by limitless credit and a rising asset base (real estate) inflated by the same expansion of credit, all extended by a State propelled by the need for the sort of domestic economic growth which maintains political support for the State's leadership elites.

Now that game has expired as the advanced-economy consumers finally reached the limits of their ability to service their rapidly expanding debts. Even the U.S. government's massive meddling and the printing/borrowing of trillions of dollars is not re-inflating the real estate bubble, and thus there is no collateral left to support the limitless credit global capital now requires for growth.

Predatory global Capitalism is thus facing a crisis of unprecedented scale and scope: the globalization/colonization "escape" from overcapacity has come to a dead end.

While some eternally hopeful capitalists look to the former colonies of Africa as the growth engine for global capitalism, a quick look at the capacity of China and Asia to produce goods quickly reveals that hope as baseless: if we add up the remaining production in the West and developed East Asia with China's monumental new capacity, we find that the global capacity outstrips all potential demand.

The world could easily ship 20 million new autos year to Africa, but unfortunately for the advanced capitalist nations, there isn't enough income in Africa to support 100 million autos and the vast infrastructure they require. The same can be said of the billion impoverished residents of China and India. Global capital would be delighted to sell them all its surplus production but for the sad fact they have no money or collateral on which to base consumer borrowing.

Now that the global real estate bubble has burst, global capital is facing a real dilemma: it has colonized and exploited virtually every populace available, and there is no one left to exploit. Their lackeys in the governments have eliminated moral hazard (that is, go ahead and speculate wildly, we'll save you all regardless of risk or the size of your losses) and expanded credit exponentially, but never-ending exponential growth is simply not possible.

And so now with the destruction of the bogus real estate bubble and speculative "wealth," global capital has screeched to a halt at the edge of an abyss it has avoided for a hundred years. Finally, there is no place left to sell overproduction, and the domestic populaces it depends on for political support are restive as they sense the ground beneath their "prosperity" has fallen away.

Thus global capital is desperately demanding the State print/borrow trillions of dollars in a futile effort to either inflate new bubbles or reinflate speculative bubbles which have popped. The reinflation will fail, even as they push governments into insolvency and fail to save Neoliberal capitalism.

Globalization also has a host of other pernicious features.

1. Concentration of resources and political power. Global capital, armed with virtually unlimited access to capital via the capital markets and various exotic instruments such as derivatives, can always outbid local owners/capitalists for resources. Once the forest, oil field, etc. is owned (or joint-ventured with local crony capitalists or Oligarch families) then it is promptly stripped/exploited/depleted.

2. Minimal accountability for environmental damage. Any environmental damage that results is of no consequence because the local political Elite can be bought for relatively modest sums. There is no profit in cleaning up the site and so to do so would be "irrational" in a rational-market metric.

Perhaps this distance from the environmental consequences of resource/wealth extraction is globalization's most pernicious feature. Mine owners never live near the tailings, and the coal plant's owners never live downwind of the sooty plume, either.

The more distant the owner, the less accountable they are for local consequences.

In today's Internet-savvy world, global capital places some modest value on corporate image, and thus a facsimile of environmental concern is made and then hyped via company propaganda. In a handful of cases, wise stewardships is not just a propaganda talking point; but the circumstances behind these exceptions are not easily codified.

3. Redistribution of income to capital from labor or local ownership is "necessary" to encourage "investment." Even in Empire States like the U.S., foreign capital is given numerous tax loopholes and other redirections of income to capital. This is always explained as necessary to encourage "investment."

But this greater income did not appear out of thin air; it was redistributed from labor and local owners via tax loopholes and credits. But since global capital is driven to seek the highest returns possible, the income extracted from Locale A is rarely reinvested in Locale A. This justification for the income redistribution--to encourage "investment"--is thus a cover for resource/profit extraction.

In the U.S., global companies like General Motors have received taxpayer bailouts in the tens of billions, supposedly to keep their production and workforce in the U.S., when the demand of global capital for higher returns forces the company to expand in Brazil at the expense of domestic U.S. jobs.

In one sense, the company has no choice. It must deploy its remaining capital at the highest return or simply close down. In the Chinese model the State owns the factories and continues to operate them at a loss. But as China's own state-owned enterprises show, permanent losses are simply not sustainable, even for the government.

4. As middle class jobs are cut, demand falls, exacerbating overcapacity. Global capital shifts away from high cost production (except where that opportunity is limited by the State), replacing middle class employment in advanced economies with lower-cost labor in less-developed economies.

Ironically, this lowers demand for the global companies' goods even as their overseas capacity expands. The net result is that financial speculation becomes an increasingly attractive use for capital. Thus selling consumers credit with which to buy cars becomes more profitable than selling them cars. Additional profit is reaped by bundling these consumer loans into packages--securitization--and selling the newly minted securities to credulous investors around the world.

Thus speculative leveraged credit and securitization can vastly increase profits even as production falls.

5. As its own income falls, the middle class follows the lead of global capital by increasingly relying on credit-based speculation rather than production for income. No one is more anxious to pursue speculative gains than someone whose income from labor is declining. Thus homeowners or prospective homeowners were delighted to follow global capital's forays into credit-based real estate speculation.

Unfortunately, speculation is no substitute in the long run for producing actual goods and services, and once the exponential blow-off was reached and the bubble popped, global capital simply sold off (or got bailed out) and moved on, while the middle class speculators were left with staggering losses in real wealth or capital traps (assets declining in value which could not be sold).

6. Due to its global nature, capital is no longer accountable for the consequences of its choices. Here's how it works: global capital gets huge tax credits (incentives that are basically nothing more than redistribution of income from labor and local entrepreneurs to global capital) for "investing" in the local economy. It then mines the local labor and/or resources of profits until overcapacity or depletion strikes. Then it shutters the factory or mine and moves its machinery elsewhere, leaving the local economy a shambles. Next it hypes the need for "investment" elsewhere, moving production to wherever offers the highest tax benefits, the least environmental restrictions and the lowest labor costs. Final step: repeat.

From the point of view of global capital, this is "obviously" the only model which "works." Local residents, workers and small-scale enterprise owners will disagree once their locale has been strip-mined of profits and wealth.

In sum: globalization is a key driver in the end of paying work and the impoverishment of local labor, resources and enterprise via the redistribution of profits and income to global capital.

The State's Vain Attempt to Distribute Systemic Risk to Taxpayers: The Yellowstone Analogy

Neoliberal refers to a model of State-managed capitalism which has been in vogue since the Great Depression and the Keynesian revolution: when capitalism's business cycle veers into discomfort (unemployment, slowing sales, etc.) then the State (government) suppresses recession with monetary policy (making money cheap and abundant) and fiscal policy (quantitative easing, injections of liquidity, stimulus programs, etc.)

That sounds just ducky, but the Yellowstone Analogy reveals the flaw in this suppression strategy. Free market capitalism's normal business cycle of over-investment and excessive risk-taking is naturally followed by a reduction in debt, the liquidation of bad loans and excess inventory, a trend to reduced risk, etc.--in other words, a fast-burning forest fire which incinerates all the deadwood, clearing space for the next generation of growth.

For decades, the operative theory of forestry management was that limited controlled burns-- mild reductions of dead underbrush and debris--would essentially reduce the possibility of a major fire to near-zero.

But the practice actually allowed a buildup of deadwood that then fueled the devastating forest fire which swept Yellowstone National Park in 1988. Various revisionist views sprouted up later, claiming the fire was not the result of misguided attempts to limit natural forces.

Now we're in a financial conflagration which is widely considered the result of failed risk-suppression policies. All the derivatives originated and sold were supposed to, along with "self-regulating markets" (smirk), limit the risks in the financial systems to near-zero.

In other words, even as dead branches piled ever higher, various complex hedges would insure no fire in the FIRE economy would ever spread.

But this private and public risk suppression not only failed to eradicate risk--it enabled risk to grow to unprecedented levels.

Globally, the State has responded to this failure to suppress risk by creating gigantic new risks and transferring them to taxpayers and buyers of government-issued debt.

The suppression technique being pursued by governments everywhere is simple: borrow and print staggering sums of money to bail out the private-sector banks which sparked the crisis, and then borrow and print even more money and throw it into the economy in an attempt to match the fiscal stimulus of World War Two spending.

Unfortunately, this stimulus is essentially adding more deadwood to an already vast pile that is already choking what's left of the economy's living forest. Without a write-off of bad debts and risky failed gambles and a closure of overcapacity, the new business cycle cannot take root.

Isn't it obvious that by trying to make forest fires a thing of the past, you're actually killing the forest?

The same mechanism is at work in the multi-trillion dollar attempts to make financial cycles of over-indebtedness and excessive risk a thing of the past.

The financial firestorm of 2008 burned off some of the deadwood, but it left no clearing. Thus the smoldering embers will set fire to all the new bad debt and deadwood blanketing the floor of our economy and a new round of monetary easing and fiscal stimulus will be attempted.

You can't make people who are already over-indebted take on more debt, and you can't make people whose collateral is falling creditworthy. To shove more debt into the system is to pile more deadwood onto the already-dense pile of dry debris littering every inch of the economy.

The big conceit here is that borrowing trillions of dollars is risk-free as long as the government is doing the borrowing.

That is an illusion--there is always risk when you borrow or print or "backstop"/guarantee trillions of dollars of risky debt; the risk has simply been transferred to taxpayers, who will soon suffer the consequences.

For the crisis in capitalism is not just debt-based--it's also resource and demographic-based.

Here in the U.S., the Social Security system will soon reverse its long trend of generating a surplus and as a result it will start adding to a Federal budget deficit that's already running $2 trillion a year.

Medicare is even more fragile, and thus we can easily foresee a fiscal crisis looming in which the Federal government can no longer borrow enough trillions to fund these entitlements. And despite all the repeated soothing official assurances, the crisis is not in 2035--it will hit in 2015 or perhaps even earlier.

This is a classic example of the *Trend Extrapolation Trap*. Back when the Social Security system was designed, it was assumed there would always be 10 workers to "pay as you go" to support 1 retiree. The Baby Boom in the 1950s made that projection reassuringly long-term--or so it seemed.

Now that we're approaching a worker-retiree ratio of 2.5-to-1, the system cannot possibly pay the benefits promised without borrowing trillions of dollars each and every year--and from whom?

Meanwhile, oil has plummeted in a long-anticipated head-fake in which global recession cuts demand, masking the arrival of Peak Oil. Will there be enough oil to fuel 100 million new Tata minicars in India plus run the 600 million existing vehicles currently burning oil? And exactly where will the electricity come from to charge up 100 million plug-in hybrid cars made by China's BYD? (Not to mention the lithium-ion batteries.)

As for all the alternative fuels, well, maybe, but right now all alternative energy sources provide 3% of global energy.

Ramping up alternative energy from 3% to 30% of global energy production will be stupendously costly--and aren't governments vacuuming up much of the world's capital to squander it on their financial sectors and local government pork-barrel projects?

Neoliberal capitalism is in crisis for one fundamental reason: the State has played "the fixer" with monetary and fiscal policy in the belief that risk could be suppressed by spreading it over the entire taxpaying populace.

But the excesses of credit, risk, leverage and overcapacity are now gutting the very middle class which the State relies on to pay most of the taxes. And as tax revenues dry up, entitlement spending ramps ever higher and borrowing is no longer cheap or even possible, then the State and the "private sector capitalism" which depended on passing off its risks and gambles-gone-awry to the State will find the firestorm was not suppressed-- it was only delayed--and not for long.

The best explanation of systemic financial risk and why it cannot be "disappeared" is The (Mis)behavior of Markets: A Fractal View of Risk, Ruin, and Reward by Benoit Mandelbrot.

The demographics trends which are about to overwhelm entitlements programs are described in Fewer: How the New Demography of Depopulation Will Shape Our Future and The Coming Generational Storm: What You Need to Know about America's Economic Future.

Perverse Incentives and the Substitution of Low-Risk Fantasy for Reality

The crisis of Neoliberal capitalism cannot be fully understood unless we grasp three mechanisms:

1. Perverse Incentives: Simulacra of value are substituted for real-world productivity making unproductive speculation, cronyism, deliberate fraud, and deception by design preferable because one can profit without any "skin in the game." Accountability becomes either an impediment or a sucker's proposition. This is reinforced by modes of thinking and plans of action which socialize losses and privatize gains, shifting of risk to taxpayers, and encouraging state-banker-dealer collusion.

2. Rational Disincentives: The gradual punishment (in relative terms) and destruction of support for production, integrity and accurate accounting places people who pursue these principles at a competitive disadvantage. When deployment of capital for speculation (i.e. unearned capital gains) is taxed at half the rate of production (i.e. earned income), then productivity is disincentivized. Unregulated "creative" accounting puts honest business at a disadvantage. Inflated earnings and hidden liabilities both make a company appear more profitable, and create competitive pressure toward collusion and deliberate fraud. The "rational" weight of various disincentives for honest and healthy commercial exchange buoys the market rationality for risky speculation.

3. The Substitution of Low-Risk Fantasy for Reality. These perverse incentives--propagated not just by financial and regulatory structures but by the mass media/marketing system described above-- led the American citizenry to believe this simulacrum of value could be a low-risk, productive, "rich" way of life. Since simulacra require complicity, we might ask why the motto of the age became "If it sounds to good to be true, it MUST be true."

Part of the answer lies in the apparently low-risk ease of profiting from real estate and financial speculation. Since organisms are selected to avoid undue risk (that is, investing significant assets and time in projects with unknown outcomes) and favor the security of the status quo, then the appeal of a seemingly secure, low-risk system which offered vast profits via leverage was overpoweringly "obvious." That it was all a fantasy was clearly visible, but the rewards were so high that the American people willingly substituted a fantasy for reality.

Chapter Three: Over-Reach and Inequality

Our situation can be summarized thusly:

1. All civil societies develop Elites; this is the nature of social animals. Elites are self-organizing groups which share the same self-interests, that is, a higher-order clique; they are not conspiracies or formal organizations.

2. Under certain conditions, the structural obstacles/negative feedbacks which constrain Elite dominance weaken and the Elites (private and public/State), like any other human group, seek to exploit the resulting windfall.

3. This leads the Elites to over-reach which creates positive feedback: the more wealth and influence the Elites/State control, the easier it becomes to control even more. The net result is the Elites and the State's share of the national income rises to historic extremes.

4. Regardless of the exact nature of over-reach--expansionist warfare or financial leverage and looting are two popular choices--the interests of the Elites and the society as a whole diverge. As this divergence grows, the social contract between the Elites and those whose productivity powers the economy and society begins fraying.

5. Over-reach ontologically (inherently) leads to structural imbalances which then threaten to destabilize the productive middle class which supports the Elites. Due to the overwhelming power of the Elites/State partnership's fiefdoms, structural reform is impossible (see Chapter Twenty below).

6. As the productive middle class's share of national income shrinks, a well-concealed, *opaque parallel system of dominance* with a structure of its own arises to exclusively serve the interests of the Plutocracy/State Elites (apparatchiks). The hidden mechanisms are many: backroom deals, unwritten "understandings," price-fixing and other forms of collusion; "gifts and donations;" political favoritism (special admission to elite public universities for the well-connected); and a cornucopia of financial benefits: access to initial public offerings, special tax laws written to reward a particular enterprise or cartel, and so on.

7. The State, which was intended as a bulwark against the natural dominance of concentrated private capital and Monarchy, has instead become the handmaiden of the rentier-financial Power Elites. The Elites and the State have thus become partners in the task of diverting ever-

larger shares of the national income to their own coffers.

8. As a result, inequality--as measured by shares of the national income and wealth--widens, furthering the divergence of interests between the productive class and the Elites/States' unproductive fiefdoms and dependents.

9. The State/Elites seek to counter these growing imbalances by extracting more from the productive class via taxes and "theft by other means" and masking this rising inequality by manipulating the politics of experience via relentless mass media propaganda.

The goal is four-fold: nurture complacency and fatalism in the citizenry; divert their attention from the concealed parallel system that benefits the Plutocracy and State Elites exclusively; legitimize simulacrum democracy and delegitimize protest.

10. To keep the State dependents passive and unthreatening, the Elites/State placate this class with "bread and circuses," State-funded entitlements paid for by raising taxes on the dwindling productive class. Under the guise of entitlements, the State (and the Elites who control it) has in effect bought the passive complicity of its dependents in the Elites' growing dominance of national income and wealth.

11. Having over-promised entitlements to the unproductive and garnered the majority of national income and wealth for themselves, the Plutocracy/State Elites can only tax the productive class so much lest they kill the horse they ride so majestically. Their only alternative to loss of income and power is to debauch the currency by printing money and debauch credit by borrowing far in excess of what can possibly be paid back.

12. The debauchery of credit and currency and rising inequality continues in a process of devolution until a phase shift/tipping point is reached and the status quo collapses in insolvency.

This process is both post-Marxism (that is, occurring outside the framework of Marxist theory) and post-Neoliberal State Capitalism--in other words, these broad intellectual frameworks failed to predict or account for the coming devolution and collapse of the State/rentier-monopoly capital Power Elite partnership.

The grand experiment of the State controlling the private economy has failed.

Both the Marxist/Socialist model of government control and ownership and the Neoliberal State Capitalist model of the State controlling the economy via monetary and fiscal manipulations have failed, for in each model there is no negative feedback to State over-reach and expansion.

In the Marxist Model, there is no negative feedback to limit *extreme concentrations of power* via State control and ownership of national assets and income. As the State Elites gorge on the national wealth (windfall exploitation), the State's interests radically diverge from those of the citizenry.

In Neoliberal State Capitalism, there is no negative feedback to limit State manipulation of monetary and fiscal inputs (i.e. borrow and/or print money). In theory, the global bond market should act as a counterforce to fiscal over-reach (excessive State debt and spending), but as recent events have shown, the U.S. is effectively unhindered by market forces: the U.S. Treasury sells bonds to primary bond dealers, the Federal Reserve creates money out of thin air, and a few days after the bond auction the Fed buys the Treasury bonds from the dealers.

The circle is complete: when the State creates money to buy its own debt, it establishes a simulacrum of an "open market" which in reality is utterly opaque and manipulated by the financial Elites and State to maintain their wealth and power.

But such perfection in positive feedback (there are no restraints on the State's ability to print, borrow and spend money) leads not to stability but to instability and collapse.

Exacerbating this devolution and eventual collapse are unprecedented external pressures on increasingly vulnerable FEW resources (food, energy and water) and infrastructure: fossil fuel depletion, environmental/soil degradation, fragile supply chains, etc., all of which increase the probabilities of chronic shortages and the geopolitical conflicts which historically arise from those shortages.

At this juncture it is important to recall that any State/government is in essence a luxury that can only exist if an economy generates a substantial surplus.

No surplus, no government. Thus subsistence-level societies do not have stand-alone governments because there is not enough surplus food to feed essentially unproductive members of the society (government). Security and other community needs are provided gratis by the group itself as a form of mutual protection/benefit. The wealthy share their surplus in exchange for status ("potlatch").

As measured by fiscal and trade deficits, the U.S. economy has not produced a sustained surplus for decades.

We have consumed far more than we have produced, and borrowed the difference from nations that have generated surplus capital and goods.

The mass media/think-tank/State propaganda machine produces reams of material claiming to "prove" that this stupendous borrowing is not just sustainable but that it is in everyone's best interests.

But the "surplus" the U.S. is trading for tangible goods and capital is paper money and future promises to pay--both essentially worthless. At some point the fraud at the heart of this exchange of "value" will be revealed and the U.S. State and Elites will be reduced to depending on the actual tangible surplus generated by the U.S. economy.

This sharp reduction of available capital to spend will trigger collapse of the over-leveraged, over-indebted, credit-dependent status quo, which requires trillions of dollars in borrowed capital to support its gargantuan State and Elites.

It is also important to recall that relative inequality in national income and wealth rises and falls in long cycles, and changes are triggered by national crisis.

I previously noted that inequality was rather low in Colonial America and then rose as the U.S. industrialized. One result of the Great Depression was the decline of inequality, which enabled the post-World War II era of rising middle class wealth and income.

Thus it is entirely within historic norms to foresee a national crisis (insolvency) which results in dramatic declines of inequality--that is, the share of national income and wealth currently diverted to the Elites and State will drop precipitously. Since national income is a zero-sum game, this decline in equality means the productive classes' share of national income will rise--put another way, they will keep the income that is being transferred to the rentier/financial and State Elites in the present era of extreme inequality.

This implies the State's role as handmaiden/servant to the rentier-financial Elites will collapse along with State finances. Given the lack of negative feedback on the State's expansion and the positive feedback of printing and spending fiat money, there is no other possible end-state but collapse/insolvency.

Let's examine our era's extreme inequality in more detail.

According to a recent (July 2009) *Wall Street Journal* analysis of Social Security Administration data, the top 6% of wage earners (high-caste) take home 1/3 of the national wage/salary income ($2.1 trillion of the $6.4 trillion in total U.S. pay in 2007); when bonuses, stock options and other non-wage income are included, the percentage rises to approximately 50%. The high-caste share of national income has been rising at approximately double the rate of average workers. Over time, this differential enabled the top 6%'s share to rise from 28% of total income to 33% in just a few years. Thus inequality is rising quickly in the current status quo.

The top 1% of households own 2/3 of the productive wealth of the nation. This number is not static, of course; the gap between the top 1% and the 99% below is widening rapidly. Congressional Budget Office data show that between 1979 and 2006, the before-tax income of the top 1 percent of U.S. households increased by 226 percent, on average (after adjusting for inflation), compared to an increase of just 15 percent for families in the middle fifth of the income spectrum (the middle class).

The after-tax income of the top 1 percent of households increased by 256 percent, after adjusting for inflation, compared to an increase of 21 percent for families in the middle income quintile. The effective federal tax rate for the top 1 percent of households — i.e., the share of their *taxable income* that they owe in taxes — fell substantially, from 37 percent to 31.2 percent As a result, the share of the nation's total after-tax income going to the top 1 percent of households more than doubled, from 7.5 percent in 1979 to 16.3 percent in 2006.

While non-taxable income statistics are hard to come by, we know that the vast majority of tax-free municipal bonds are owned by the top 5% of households, and that the vast majority of Elite wealth is protected from taxes by family and estate trusts, funds and income held overseas and a multitude of other tax avoidance schemes (legal and quasi-legal) unavailable to middle class households. The vast majority of the Elite's income is unearned, that is, not wages but rents, dividends, capital gains, etc., which are either taxed at lower rates or subject to other tax avoidance strategies.

Thus the top 1%'s share of total national income (nontaxable or protected from taxation as well as taxable) is more on the order of a third. (Approximately 60% of the income-generated wealth of the nation-- rents protected by depreciation, dividends, interest, capital gains, tax-free bond income, non-taxable trust income, etc.-- flows to the top 1%. Thus wages/salaries/taxable income is a poor measure of total wealth and income.)

Historically, this concentration of wealth and income is an extreme for this nation. The State (all government, state, county, city, semi-autonomous public agencies, transit authorities, public universities, etc.) currently absorbs approximately 40% of the nation's GDP, also an extreme. (The Federal government absorbs about 20% of GDP.)

We should also note that the rise of entitlements/dependency has occurred in parallel with rising inequality/ever greater share of national income diverted to the State and Plutocracy; the skyrocketing cost of "pay as you go" entitlements is thus paid with borrowed money and higher taxes on the dwindling productive middle class, leaving the Plutocracy and State fiefdoms' shares of the national income intact.

None of this is common knowledge, for the corporate Elite owns the highly concentrated mass media, and it would not serve their interest for this sort of data to be widely disseminated in the mass media.

Given that elites form in all societies with any surplus, the notion of eradicating Elites entirely is impractical.

Clearing away old Elites (liquidating, murdering or imprisoning them on the Soviet, Chinese or Cambodian models) has merely provided opportunities for a new Elite to take the place of the old Elite.

But reducing extreme inequality by restricting the diversion of the productive classes' earnings to the Elite/State partnership is not just entirely possible but it has recent historical precedent (the rapid drop in inequality 1940 - 1970).

It is important to note that eras of relatively low inequality have generally been the most widely prosperous, stable and creative in American history.

As noted elsewhere in this analysis, the U.S. Constitution does not restrict the growth of Elites or the State, nor does it contain any mechanism to limit the concentration of their wealth, power and influence. The Elites effectively control all three branches of the U.S. government and so the "balance of powers" is ineffective in limiting the rise of inequality. It is up to the citizenry to limit rising inequality; the structure of government itself only feeds an ever-enlarging State.

Having noted this, we must also note that the U.S. Constitution does not restrict the reduction of inequality, either. The Constitution is itself neutral; if the citizenry allow the Elites and State to dominate the national income, media and the politics of experience, then the Constitution is powerless to obstruct this concentration of power.

Recall that the State and its fiefdoms have no inherent interest in limiting their own reach, income and influence; rather, the State is ontologically constructed to seek a greater share of national income and ever greater influence and control--just like the private-sector Elites which partner with the State.

Put another way: there is no negative feedback to restrict the growth of the State except an engaged, skeptical citizenry which demands and enforces transparency and accountability. This will require new negative feedback loops and strengthening existing regulatory feedbacks that have been reduced to simulacra.

Thus no revolution is necessary; indeed, nothing illegal is required, either. Opting out is perfectly legal, as is constructing an alternative transparent, fully accountable economy and society which will prosper even as the financial Elites and the State collapse in insolvency.

Chapter Four: Insurmountable Barriers to Structural Reform

In a perfect world, both the citizenry and those grasping the reins of power would conclude that serious structural reform would serve their long-term interests better than structural collapse. Yet there are ontological (and therefore insurmountable) barriers to any such reform, obstacles which can perhaps best be understood as forces of nature similar to gravity: to expect any concentration of political and financial power to relinquish its power rather than defend it is akin to expecting gravity to cease its pull on mass.

Elites, by definition, hold concentrations of wealth and control at immensely higher *power densities* than the broad non-elite populace. I term this structural imbalance in power density *asymmetric stakes in the game*, in which the game is the concentration and distribution of national income and wealth, both via State-collected taxes and private capital.

To better understand the concept of *power density*, in which power is financial and political, let's compare a rural, agricultural economy such as the U.S. circa 1783 and a post-industrial urbanized economy such as the U.S. in 2009.

Setting aside the issue of slavery in 1783 America--from one point of view, a forced concentration of labor to serve the plantation model of production--we note the diffusion of power in the non-slave states. Voters--the ultimate source of political compliance and thus power--and private and public financial assets were diffused except for a few (by today's standards modest) urban centers: Philadelphia, Boston and New York. What Marx called "the means of production"--the capital, plant, tools and knowledge required to produce goods and services and thus wealth--were spread over the rural and urban populations alike.

Another way of describing this diffusion of power is to calculate the rate of concentration via the rate of inequality.

Thus a feudal society in which an Elite holds most of the wealth has a high rate of inequality, where a populace of free small landowners and tradespeople has a low level of inequality.

Non-slaveowning Colonial America had a low, stable rate of inequality, a condition which has plentiful academic documentation. According to Frank Ackerman's The Political Economy of Inequality, the top 1% of free adult males held 12% of the wealth in 1774 and 29% in 1860. The share of the top 10% rose from 49% in 1774 to 73% in 1860.

As the North industrialized and the Southern plantation-based economy consolidated, then wealth inequality increased between the Revolution and the Civil War. This concentration of wealth continued unabated through the Gilded Age up to 1929, when the Great Depression wrought vast increases in State powers as wealth was widely destroyed. The net result was a much lower level of inequality from 1940 through the early 1970s--not coincidentally, the era of true prosperity for the middle class and the alleviation of extremes of poverty.

As described above, this true prosperity faded in the stagflation and ennui of the 1970s and was replaced with a credit/debt bubble-based simulacrum of prosperity which masked the diversion of national wealth and income to Elites-- a pseudo-prosperity which is now imploding.

Mass industrial/technical production owned and distributed by global corporations arose from the great efficiencies and profits created by concentrating capital, materials, transport, expertise and labor into monopolies/cartels. Fighting and winning a global war (World War II) greatly expanded the U.S. government's reach and size. These concentrations of capital, expertise, logistics, labor and control created fiefdoms of the State and a private-sector Plutocracy which partnered to extend a mutually beneficial global empire of so-called "soft power" influence and "hard power" military dominance.

Wealth and thus power is now extremely concentrated; at least 2/3 of the productive (income-producing) wealth and 60% of the income-generated wealth of the U.S. is held by 1% of the populace. (According to an analysis by the *New York Times* and Simon Cay Johnson, the top 400 taxpayers' tax rate was 17%--and that, recall, is on taxable income of $250 million each on average, a sum which is only a percentage of their total income, much of which is sheltered.)

From the long view, the cycle of wealth concentration has again reached an apex similar to that of 1929. The primary difference between 1929 and the present some 80 years hence is that the State has greatly concentrated its power and share of the national income.

Perhaps coincidentally but perhaps not, this cycle of extreme inequality aligns extremely well with the 80-year generational cycle described in the full *Survival+*.

The Grand Failure of Government to Limit Concentration of Power

While much is made of the "balance of powers" in the U.S. and other democracies--the power of the executive branch being offset by the legislative and judicial branches--this "balance" completely failed to hinder the credit/housing bubble and the structural fraud and embezzlement at its heart. No branch of the "balanced powers of the State" saw any reason to interfere with the systemic looting and debauchery of credit and currency.

We should also note that in previous periods of extreme concentrations of wealth and high inequality, the "balanced powers" of the U.S. government did not reverse or even seriously challenge these long periods of high inequality. In this sense we should be careful not to overestimate the State's control over wealth concentration and rising inequality.

Despite the supposedly "leveling influence" of income taxes, wealth has become ever more concentrated in the past 40 years, paralleling the high inequality between the Civil War and the Great Depression. Neither the "trust-busting" actions of the Federal government in the early 1900s nor the rise of industrial unions reversed or disrupted the 1860-1930 period of high wealth concentration/high inequality.

This, then, is the *grand failure of government*: due to the concentrations of power accumulated by those with *asymmetric stakes in the game*, any attempt to limit a concentration of power is thwarted by the status quo. All the issues which so worried Madison in The Federalist Papers have come to full flower: the power of the State has been legally channeled into Elites which have nothing to fear from any branch of the State because they are the State.

Despite decades of attempted electoral "reform," elections in the U.S. grow ever more prohibitively expensive, and it is still legal to contribute large sums of money to politicians. The cliche has it that "money is the mothers' milk of politics" and as has been noted above, it is far cheaper to buy a legislative loophole than it is to pay taxes, build treatment plants, relinquish monopoly, etc.

These concentrations of financial and thus political power flow ontologically from the concentrations of capital and labor that were necessary to industrial production.

The model of a "factory" mass-producing goods, so successful in manufacture, has been applied, consciously or unconsciously, to fields of endeavor which are structurally quite different from manufacture--education, for instance, with the mixed results one would expect of misapplied models.

The human mind's power comes from understanding models and applying them to new situations. In the long view, it is understandable that just as Newtonian physics sparked a frenzy of misapplied models (the human being understood as a mechanical device like a clock, etc.), so too would the highly successful model of concentrated mass-production be earnestly and enthusiastically misapplied.

This concentration of materials, machinery, transport, labor and capital--the factory and the industrial corporation--naturally led to a concentration of organized labor, a model which, now that industrial production has faded, has been misapplied to the last outsized concentration of labor: government.

With no real restraints on government largesse, then public-union labor has concentrated its political power and "won" (I use quotation marks because there has never been any real negative feedback to its concentration of power) stupendous benefits and wages which have created the "upper-caste" I have described above: a protected class of technocrats/apparatchiks who are compensated at two or three times (when pension and healthcare benefits are included) the market rates earned by their lower-caste private-sector brethren.

Once financial and political power has become concentrated into monopoly-capital cartels and State fiefdoms, then those Elites hold highly *asymmetric stakes in the game*: they have so much more to gain and lose from the political distribution of taxes and exemptions from regulation than non-Elites that they will fiercely deploy all their power and wealth to preserve and extend their share of the national income.

In contrast, the non-Elite citizenry have vanishingly modest stakes in the tax-distribution games; while a narrowly focused tax law will enrich an Elite for decades to come, the consequences to the broad non-Elite citizenry are so diffused as to be akin to the brush of a feather.

Immense State/Elite empires have been constructed from initially modest taxes collected from tens of millions of non-Elites--Medicare, for example--while seemingly minor tax laws have enabled vast empires of private capital to solidify. For example, energy, where fortunes have been built on depletion allowances and other tax schemes far more favorable than those awarded to manufacturers, and real estate, where depreciation hides vast rivers of income behind the perverse idea that a building rising in real value is magically declining in worth.

From its humble tax-funded beginnings, Medicare has grown into a stupendously profitable empire which will soon exceed both the military-intelligence complex (the Pentagon) and the Social Security system in budget. This vast empire is comprised of loosely allied fiefdoms (the AMA, trial lawyers, pharmaceutical, insurance and hospital industries, etc.), each eager to defend its turf from non-Elite interference and the encroachment of the other fiefdoms.

The State's apparatchiks have gained income and power along with their private-sector partners, and thus rather than provide a negative feedback counterforce to this concentration of wealth and income, the State is in effect a positive feedback, furthering the concentration of wealth and power into Elite hands.

State Monopolies: Violence, Conscription, Taxation and Inflation

The State itself of course holds monopolies on a handful of powers that are concentrated indeed: the dispensation of "legitimate" violence, the power to conscript citizens to fight wars (legally declared or otherwise), the power to tax the citizenry and lastly, the terrible power to rob the citizenry by means of inflation and/or currency devaluation, what I term *theft by other means*.

Economist John Maynard Keynes quipped, "By a continuing process of inflation, government can confiscate, secretly and unobserved, an important part of the wealth of their citizens." This is theft by other means.

Why does the State seek to steal its citizens' wealth via inflation? The politics of inflation dictate it:

1. Politicians need to distribute swag ("free money") to the electorate every two years. Their perspective is thus necessarily short-term as no politician dares care what transpires a decade or two hence.

As a result, politicians must favor inflation, which enables them to borrow/print money and distribute it as swag to voters and Elites ("special interests") in the present and pay interest on the new debt with "cheaper" future dollars.

2. Voters possess the built-in human bias for present gain over future gain. Thus future insolvency is meaningless to those demanding State largesse in the present.

Indeed, politicians have noted that those who demand sacrifice in the present to address a long-term crisis lose elections while those who distribute swag while ignoring the gathering storm win elections.

3. Inflation is thus "good" for politicians and the State as it enables paying off obligations assumed in the present with devalued future currency. But is it "good" for the voters who actually earn income? Is a policy which robs a third of your money every decade a worthy policy? For that is precisely what "low" inflation of 2.5-3% annually does: it reduces your dollars' values by a third every decade.

Will the swag "given" to you (is it "given" when it's your own future earnings?) now in the form of government benefits and tax cuts add up to more than a third of your future earnings over a decade? Unlikely, to say the least.

4. So politicians exploit the human bias for short-term gain even as they rob the taxpayers via inflation over the long term. Inflation is tolerable as long as you're a wage earner and your income rises at the same rate as inflation.

But income from labor (wages/salaries) have been flat since the early 70s for most Americans, and so inflation has only been "good" for those holding assets which have risen in lockstep with inflation.

For those whose earnings rise nominally by 15% a decade while inflation robs 30% of their purchasing power, then "a little inflation" is a long-term disaster.

5. The usual argument in favor of inflation is debt-based. That is, inflation is wonderful because it enable us to pay off our debts with future "cheaper" dollars. But if our incomes are being robbed by inflation, then is that "benefit" of inflation really so valuable? If I lose a third of my purchasing power in a decade does being able to pay down my mortgage with depreciated dollars offset my loss of purchasing power? No--unless my mortgage payment exceeds my income by a fair margin, which is essentially impossible.

6. Deflation is excellent for those with cash and earnings and awful for kleptocracy governments and those with over-leveraged debt. The entire idea that "inflation is good" masks a perverse incentive: take on as much debt as you possibly can because interest will become "cheaper"

to pay in the future (assuming your earnings keep up with inflation).

If your earnings don't keep up with inflation, well, too bad.

7. The government's "earnings" are tax revenues. As profits and incomes have fallen, so have tax revenues. So as the purchasing power of its taxpayers' wages are stolen via inflation--"theft by other means"-- then the State's ability to collect ever-larger sums of money via taxes is crimped. Unless, of course, the government can create asset bubbles via loose credit and unlimited liquidity which then generate huge capital gains which can then be taxed.

8. To distribute swag to voters and Elites, the State kleptocracy offloads the payments into the future. By creating inflation then the State guarantees (or so it reckons) that it will be able to pay the interest on that debt with "cheaper" money collected from taxpayers in the future.

But as taxpayers find the purchasing power of their earnings declining (*theft by other means*) then they respond to the incentives presented by the government: borrow to the hilt and speculate in asset bubbles as the only way left to maintain purchasing power.

This dependence by both State and citizenry on asset bubbles to maintain purchasing power leads to over-leverage and over-indebtedness which then leads inevitably to a collapse of asset values (which were based on exponential credit expansion) and the tax revenues which were dependent on asset bubbles.

Now the taxpayers find their post-bubble assets decimated and their purchasing power diminished while government finds its tax revenue base has been gutted. Paying interest on all that debt while distributing unlimited swag was predicated on rising tax revenues. That plan has now been revealed as fantasy.

Interestingly, the original Constitution did not explicitly grant powers of conscription or monetary debasement. Yet the vaunted "balance of powers" has not impeded the State from concentrating monetary powers in order to reward Elites and steal not just from its present citizens but even its future citizens.

But even the State cannot control the cycle of over-indebtedness, collapsing asset values and the impoverishment of its people via inflation. The end-state is insolvency, and as the State's monopolies fail to sustain the status quo then its various Elites will battle each other for the remaining spoils: what I term *internecine conflict between protected fiefdoms.*

Internecine Conflict Between Protected Fiefdoms

"Internecine" has an interesting and highly relevant history. The Latin source of the word, a derivative of the verb "to kill," meant "fought to the death, murderous, as in "all the way, to the death." Samuel Johnson defined the word in the 18th century as "endeavoring mutual destruction." The word has now come to mean "relating to internal struggle."

These meanings are the heart of my term *internecine conflict between protected fiefdoms* because they describe how the various fiefdoms, though protected from non-Elite interference by their concentrated political power, must now fight each other to the death for their share of dwindling tax revenues and weakening regulatory perquisites. Rather than accept a reduced share of tax revenues, each fiefdom will endeavor to maintain its own share by cannibalizing the share currently enjoyed by another fiefdom.

This internecine conflict will take precedence over structural transformations which would positively serve the nation as a whole (and even the Elites defending their fiefdoms). As a result, this conflict will demand ever greater resources from each fiefdom and deplete whatever limited resources could have been devoted to structural change. These internecine wars will thus hasten the collapse of the entire status quo.

Each State fiefdom and private-industry cartel which depends on the State for funding or regulatory protection (energy, healthcare, military, etc.) will be fighting a two-front war: one against the taxpaying public (the productive middle class which pays most of the taxes) from which they will be extracting higher taxes and "junk fees" and the other against competing fiefdoms.

An analogy might be a sinking ship on which the officers are fighting each other and the crew. Focused on their internecine struggles for dominance, they pay no attention to the listing deck and other signs of impending catastrophe until the ship is slipping beneath the waves.

When the partnership between the State and Plutocracy unravels, then systemic collapse is at hand.

The partnership was based on a mutually parasitical relationship: the State's elected officials depended on the largesse of the Plutocracy, which depended on the State to protect its share of the national income and wealth.

As the productive middle class opts out (having no other choice), tax revenues continue declining in a positive-feedback death-spiral: the more taxes and junk fees imposed on the remaining productive citizenry, the greater the incentive to opt out by quitting, moving to the underground economy or simply making less money and buying fewer goods.

This decline forces the State to borrow and/or print vast sums of money which eventually negatively impact the national economy on which the Plutocracy depends for much of its income. Facing drastically reduced revenues, the State finds its powers to impose regulatory and taxation schemes on the citizenry have weakened. In desperation, the State fiefdoms begin eyeing the vast reserves of Plutocratic wealth and income as untapped sources of tax revenues.

Like the middle class, the Plutocracy will increasingly view the State not as protector but as an unproductive parasite that provides less and less even as it harvests a rising share of the dwindling national income.

Once the State alienates the Plutocracy, the State's days as a solvent enterprise are numbered. The mass media will turn against the State (being owned by a handful of global corporations, the media will do its masters' bidding) and the Plutocracy will speed the global sheltering of its remaining assets and income, in effect planning to profit from the inevitable collapse of the U.S. sovereign debt and currency.

But without the State to protect it from an aroused citizenry, the Plutocracy may find itself the target of widespread ire and insurrection. Even as it follows the pathway taken by the Roman Elites as their empire crumbled--retreating to well-defended enclaves--the Plutocracy will find its own freedom of movement, capital and monopoly restricted by the State's attack on its assets and the public's awakening to the coming collapse in entitlements and other State services.

The State and Plutocracy share the same hubris: each believes there should be no limits on its own over-reach.

The irony is that once their interests diverge and the partnership crumbles, each is left too weak to control the forces unleashed by their mutual over-reach.

As states around the globe seek to borrow their way out of insolvency, private borrowing is squeezed; this intense competition for dwindling surplus global capital forces interest rates to rise to levels few anticipated. (Readers of oftwominds.com were of course fully aware of both the rising trajectory and its enduring nature.)

The Plutocracy, having engorged itself on profits reaped from the artificially low interest rates engineered by State manipulation of financial markets, will be less than pleased with the sudden disappearance of cheap surplus capital. The direct consequences of much higher rates globally--the destruction of equity, bond holdings and real estate valuations--will also negatively affect the Plutocracy's wealth and income, widening the rift between what the State fiefdoms see as in their best interests and what the Plutocracy views as in its best interests.

Even as what is understood by the State and Plutocracy as "the common good" diverge, the interests of the crumbling partnership (State and Plutocracy) are diverging from those of the general populace.

Facing the erosion or even dissolution of their concentrations of power, capital and labor, the State fiefdoms and the private-capital Elites unite in one last-ditch campaign to preserve their perquisites and shares of the national income via simulacrum reforms marketed as "preserving our institutions" (see chapter Fourteen, "Interlocking Traps").

The State and Plutocracy will never voluntarily reduce their share of the national income when simulacra of reform (funding State largesse with more debt, masking the approaching insolvency with accounting trickery, announcing bogus "grand compromises" which will save the status quo without any visible sacrifice, etc.) can put off the inevitably catastrophic consequences to a future day. When that moment finally arrives, reforms of any type will be as inconsequential as the many edicts issued in the waning days of the Roman Empire.

Asymmetric Stakes in the Game

Government, not just Federal but state, county and city, has two extraordinary powers: it can collect revenues via taxation, permits and fees, by force if necessary, and then distribute those funds however the officials in charge desire.

Theoretically, the voters can express their dissatisfaction with the decisions made every two or four years, but such referendums are inevitably diluted by distracting propaganda paid for by the Elites and high-castes who benefit most from maintaining the status quo.

I say "theoretically" for another reason: those on the receiving end of those stupendous revenues collected by the State have an *asymmetric stake in the game*: the potential losses in their own personal income are not just theoretical, they are very real, and so they mobilize their forces to protect their own fiefdom and perquisites with a frantic, desperate zeal unmatched by the voters, who have a much smaller stake in the division of tax revenues.

Thus the public employee unions, American Medical Association, pharmaceutical companies, trial lawyers, defense contractors and other Elites with asymmetric stakes funnel millions of dollars into the re-election campaigns of politicians. The net result, of course, is that the very expenses which have skyrocketed--public pensions and healthcare, to name but two--are "off the table," sacrosanct, untouchable.

For the politicians, there is an even bigger threat: should they cross the pharmaceutical industry, the AMA, the trial lawyers or any well-funded public employee union, these special interest groups will not just stop funding their campaigns--they will target them for extermination by funding an opponent.

Put yourself in the shoes of an elected official. You collect a small sum in campaign contributions from the general public--the non-Elite "little people" you are pledged to serve. You collect another larger sum from the party organs--political action committees, etc. Then you collect a sum five times greater than those two sources combined from a handful of powerful special interests that hold extremely asymmetric stakes in the game of distributing the tax swag/revenues.

Who are you going to ignore or even double-cross? Not the special interests who have funded your political power. Who you ignore or double-cross is the public, who has a small stake in every decision you make. You can count on that come election time, when an emotional issue can be blown out of proportion via propaganda to make the voters forget the "death by a thousand cuts" taxes and reductions in services they have suffered.

How many taxpayer/voters will write an angry letter to their local politician because parking fines doubled? They may grumble to friends, colleagues, et al. but they'll just pay it, fuming all the while.

How about that 1% increase to sales tax, the surcharge to the municipal water bill, the higher subway fares and the doubled fee to enter a state park? The typical voter is annoyed and frustrated by these additional taxes and fees, but it simply isn't enough money at any one time to trigger their political act of protest.

Added together, these additional taxes and fees total a stupendous sum--in the multiple billions of dollars. Yet because we "little people" pay them in small increments and only occasionally, then our stake in the game of distributing the tax swag is asymmetrically trivial compared to the players who are collecting the billions. They are playing for keeps, while we're playing—and losing--small money, again and again.

If you rounded up $100 from every neighbor, colleague, family member and other person in your own network, and walked into your local politician's office with $10,000 in a paper bag and a short list of items you wanted addressed, then you'd get a hearing.

Or if you collected 10,000 signatures to recall your local politician over these endless tax increases, then the politician would face a danger other than an desperate-for-swag special interest: an aroused, angry public who was organized to exterminate his/her political power.

But nobody ever collects the $10,000 or the 10,000 signatures of outrage--we all just pay the fines, the junk fees, the extra sales tax, the additional income tax and the higher entrance fees and passively fume. Our stake in each game of revenue enhancement is small, so we do nothing. The special interests' stake is all-or-nothing, gigantic, as important as life itself--and so they will throw their last million at the politicos in charge of the tax revenue (and revenues from the sale of bonds) and demand their fiefdom be protected at all costs.

This is how the states, counties, cities, agencies and eventually the central government become insolvent and unable to pay their increasingly unaffordable obligations.

Asymmetric Stakes in the Game is a key concept in the *Survival+* analysis because it plays out in so many fields in which wealth is collected from millions but distributed to an Elite.

The truly Kafkaesque nightmare that is the U.S. "healthcare" (actually sick-care) system is a prime example. The players who gorge themselves on the hundreds of billions of dollars in tax swag will fight to the bitter end to maintain their share of the wealth, even if it eventually causes the collapse of the entire system. That inevitability is what I term *internecine conflict between protected fiefdoms*.

Asymmetric Stakes in the Game impacts every industry which is either funded by the State (tax revenues and State borrowing) or regulated by the State--in other words, virtually every important industry. Those with the most to lose will fight for their share of the national wealth with extreme ferocity, while those paying the endless incrementally higher taxes will never reach the threshold of demanding fundamental transformation.

An asymmetric Stake in the Game also plays out in the stock and financial markets.

Millions of employees and self-employed people contribute to a 401K and/or IRA (individual retirement account), and millions of public employees contribute to pension funds. A relatively small number of money managers decide how to invest/play those billions.

A relative handful of players collect most of the winnings from that game. The millions of players (those with 401Ks, etc.) who have lost 40% of their accumulated wealth in the two years 2007- 2009 are essentially powerless (you get to move your 401K money around any of four funds, all of which lost 40%) sheep lined up to be sheared by the players with an asymmetric stake in the game.

If you and I can collect $10 million in bonuses each, while our firm can reap $40 billion and then buy political protection for a mere $100 million of that swag, are we motivated to level the playing field? Of course not. We're interested in processing as many sheep as we can, and in keeping the game rigged in our favor.

The swag from the game is so gargantuan that we will move Heaven and Earth to persuade the regulatory Powers That Be to legitimate our advantages. It's literally financial life or death for us, while the "little people" who lost 40% of their stake, well, they will just sigh and passively accept their fate; maybe they'll glance at a headline in a magazine about a new mutual fund or ETF, and that's the end of their discontent.

Though their cumulative losses in the rigged game totaled some $13 trillion between 2007 and 2009, individually each passively accepts their own losses without regard to the nature of the game. Each surrenders political power to the Elites because the losses don't seem to have a political source: **masking the political source of the asymmetry is the key to the Power Elites' success keeping the game rigged in their own favor.**

So the mainstream media dutifully spews the propaganda that the "market is a rational mechanism for price discovery" and all the rest while behind the scenes a handful of players reap $100 million a day by gaming the trading system at its very root.

This account is replayed in every industry at some level, for the concentration of regulatory reach, tax revenues and the power to distribute those revenues is irresistible to those seeking to protect or enlarge their share of the national income. Those enjoying a share of this immense swag will fight to their last breath to defend their share, while the debt-serfs paying the devilishly diffused taxes and fees are too overwhelmed, exhausted and distracted to resist or voice their objections. That is the essence of *Asymmetric Stakes in the Game*.

Illusions of Incremental Change

The State and Plutocracy respond with incremental changes (simulacra of fundamental change) which they hope will reverse the decline without affecting their power, wealth and privilege. Alas, merely adjusting the parameters in a failing system is not enough to rescue it from collapse.

The illusion of incremental change is both an appealing self-deception and a crassly conscious attempt to dissipate political discontent.

Various analogies spring to mind: a rotting bridge, to name but one. As boards rot to the threshold of breaking, then patches are made; new boards are tacked over the rotted planks to offer the illusion of repair, even as the beams and posts of the entire bridge weaken by the day. At some critical threshold (the "tipping point" or phase shift), the entire bridge collapses, "repairs" and all.

Superficial "reforms" and repairs made for show are simulacra designed to divert attention from real reforms, and thus minimize the sacrifices required by real change.

We all want to believe that our modest incremental changes will lead to fundamental transformation; but consciously or unconsciously, we select imitations of change rather than real transformation. This provides us with the comforting illusion that all our existing perquisites can continue on untouched by real change.

Believing our own self-deception, we also present these simulacra of reform as authentic in order to win the approval of others and gain a stay from real change. This blatant manipulation never strikes the originator as deceptive or fraudulent. For having convinced themselves that a facsimile of change is equivalent to true transformation, those presenting the illusions are enjoying the best of both worlds: they believe their own deceptions (and thus suffer fewer self-recriminations) and as a result their persuasive powers are enhanced when they "sell" simulacra of reform to others as real transformation.

That the bridge will collapse is not important; what is important is that it will collapse in the future, not now. That is the ultimate power of the illusion of incremental change.

The High-Cost Structure Economy

The full *Survival+* text laid out the reasons why the U.S. economy has become a high-cost, high-overhead system: marginal returns, complacency, etc. It is worth noting that together these forces have created a top-heavy economy resistant to cost-cutting. Just trimming budgets triggers internecine warfare, as noted above, but even that process does not address bureaucratic creep, endemic insurance fraud, a legal system which burdens every business with hidden costs, high taxes, an absurdly costly and inefficient healthcare system, etc.

Each layer of this systemic overhead is protected by an Elite or fiefdom with an asymmetric stake in the game, and thus each is impervious to meaningful reform. Since these high overhead costs are systemic in nature--meaning every enterprise pays high costs--then reforming any one layer, as painful as that will be, exerts a trivial reduction in overall systemic costs.

These high systemic costs constitute yet another insurmountable structural barrier to reform as they insure that whatever cost-cutting is accomplished will produce essentially trivial results despite its stupendous political cost.

Chapter Five: The Politics of Experience

The human mind makes sense of the chaotic jumble of sensory experiences and internal mental states by assembling *explanatory narratives*—what we call "stories." To the believer, the "story" "explains" how things work. In pre-scientific cultures, many such stories were not simply wrong but injurious. Thus we have cultures in which it is believed that pregnant women shouldn't eat much.

To those who believe in the ontological (i.e. inherent or a priori) efficacy and rationality of "the market," then the pricing of the last ten wild tuna on Earth via the auction block is entirely "obvious" and "natural." The notion that the eradication of a species might have some value not calculated by "the market" is sacrilege and suppressed with the same fanatic fervor as any interfaith challenge to religious authority.

Politics is consent, persuasion and power.

Humans are social animals because banding together by consent and bloodlines provides significant survival benefits over "going it alone." In its essence, politics is the granting of power to leaders for some benefit to those consenting to be led. The leaders must persuade consent or compliance, either by touting a persuasive narrative or creating a coercive system of punishment/terror.

The ultimate summary of politics is power.

In lower animals, this boils down to power over reproduction (i.e. being able to improve one's chances of passing along one's genes via choice or coercion) and food. In humans, reproduction remains key (hence every despot acquires a harem and every official a mistress) but power also includes the various fruits of civilization such as wealth and wide-ranging political powers expressed through institutions such as religion, the state, etc.

In financial terms, imposing one's will via coercion/terror is a costly affair. Maintaining a vast gulag of prisons, secret police, domestic armies, etc., drains off a tremendous share of the national wealth, and the coercive state/Empire has a nasty habit of destroying or driving away many if not most of its most productive citizenry.

Thus the "natural selection" process of the coercive state (be it monarchy, oligarchy, state or Empire) weeds out the rebellious, the skeptical and the most productive, leaving the cowed unproductive or the sullen, willfully unproductive and a huge class of dependent drones ruled by a class of overlords with few limits on what they can skim from what remains of their economy.

The better choice is to persuade the people you wish to skim from to freely offer their consent and their compliance. This is best accomplished by creating a series of narratives in which your power (and the power of your class) is "obvious," "natural" and "beneficial." Thus we have cultures of caste in which the "high-borns'" privileges and power have been accepted as the "natural order of things." All the Powers That Be need do is maintain this narrative via whatever mediums are available (the pulpit, the media, etc.) and marginalize any challenging narratives as unnatural, representing the forces of Evil, counter to our sacred way of life, etc.

As an example in the U.S., we might consider the entire narrative of debt/credit. The idea of credit has been sold as a "benefit" for the average citizen; with credit, one needn't save up for five years to buy an auto, one can drive a new car out of the lot today and enjoy it for the five years it takes to pay it off in installments (debt/credit).

All narratives with political and thus economic consequences can be best untangled by this simple question: *cui bono*, to whose benefit?

While credit "obviously" has some visible benefits to the borrower, the line between a borrower and a debt-serf can be thin indeed.

If we examine the profits generated by auto sales, we find that the profits generated by the credit/debt used to purchase the vehicle far exceed the profits made by manufacturing the vehicle. The same is true of housing and virtually all other goods.

So who benefits from an economy based on credit? Everyone, we are told; but it seems some benefit more than others.

Is there any more ideal system than one in which the vast majority of citizens are so heavily indebted that they have little time or energy left to question the system that has essentially enslaved them? Their high indebtedness generates a constant stream of heavy profits while their overworked, anxiety-ridden lifestyle ensures that political challenges to the Powers That Be will be stillborn or easily shunted aside as the ravings of cranks and doomsayers.

For one of the most powerful narratives in America is that we must always be positive and upbeat. One of the easiest ways to dismiss a critic in any setting is to label him or her a "doomsayer." "Just get with the program": that is, put your nose to the grindstone, make your debt payments and shut up.

Another powerful narrative with immense political consequences is the casting of 24/7 "entertainment" as a positive benefit to the masses. To be offered a cornucopia of distraction at any hour—what could be better? What could be better, indeed, for keeping a populace too distracted to question the "obvious" narratives which shape their compliance to debt-serf servitude?

This is the Politics of Experience: the presentation of a narrative, a context and a "problem" framed such that the "solution" richly benefits a self-serving Elite.

For instance: as public transit agencies and school districts face insolvency, the "problem" as presented by the public employee unions is that the stingy taxpayers are not providing these essential public services with sufficient funds to operate. The "solution" is "we need more money, so raise taxes."

If this is the only "problem," then why are requests for overtime pay, directors' salaries, the average monthly pensions of retirees, the length of service required to retire, explanations for why 80% of firefighters retire on "disability," etc., met with stony silence or angry resistance? Why are analyses comparing the labor costs of operating the systems today and 30 years ago suppressed or dismissed? Because the labor costs have shot up far faster than ridership, number of students, or the underlying economy; the Elite, in this case, the "high-caste" of public employees, has enriched themselves at the expense of the no-real-wage-increase-in-30-years public.

All attempts to question the "obvious solution is we need more money" are suppressed, marginalized or attacked because revealing the actual causes of the insolvency--over-reach by State employees--would topple the narrative which supports the Elites' control and power.

In a similar way, "the market" has achieved a quasi-religious status as the perfect arbiter of efficiency and rationality. Thus the last ten wild tuna on the planet will be priced on the auction block based on their scarcity. The value of that species to humanity as a whole and the ecology of the seas is not factored by "the market's" flawless efficiency and rationality.

Or consider a small tree frog that will be extirpated by the logging of its habitat. The small frog has zero market value; as a commodity, it has no value since nobody wants to eat it or turn it into a marketable product.

But what if the skin of this frog produces a film with anti-bacteriological characteristics that might be highly valuable to humanity? "The market" has no mechanism to assess this potential or future value.

Rather than being an "efficient" or "rational" machine, the market in these cases is a blind, irrational machine that reduces all planetary inputs to a type of *scarcity-value* gravel. If you happen to profit from the trade in that gravel, it's may well appear rational and efficient. But if you recognize all that the market failed to value, not just rationally, but in any way at all, then you might see "the market" as not just irrational but so out of touch with reality as to be psychotic.

Try getting that perspective into the mass media, and you'll discover that you're the one considered psychotic and out of touch with reality. That's "the politics of experience:" narratives which support Elites' power and privileges as "obvious" and "natural" are sustained, as are "entertainments" which distract and dilute questions like cui bono; all else is marginalized, dismissed or rejected as a form of sacrilege.

R.D. Laing was a psychiatrist by training, and his understanding of the politics of experience flowed from his analysis of troubled families with "psychotic" or "insane" members. He found that in some cases, the family's "leaders" (the adults) had subconsciously selected one member of the family to bear the blame for the family's troubles and conflicts. This child was then labeled "rebellious," "uncooperative," etc., and as the child's resistance grew then they were viewed as a psychiatric case.

Laing found (along with Gregory Bateson) that when humans are given a narrative which runs counter to their own experience this disconnect forms a double-bind--an internal state of "no way out." At this point the human can slip into passivity or other states which are categorized as psychiatric "problems" to be treated with drugs.

This is not to say that all madness is essentially political, only that the resistance to irrational narratives is easily cast by those intent on preserving their own power as some sort of psychiatric "illness." The dominant narrative which supports the power structure cannot be allowed to be recognized as the "problem;" thus the beauty of a system in which rebellion, resistance or *cui bono* questioning can be cast as an "obviously" psychiatric "problem" to be "treated."

Those unable to be "processed" medically can be dismissed as "fringe" people unworthy of comment. Those who experience a double-bind between the supposedly "obvious" narratives they're expected to accept and their own internal experiences are given prescription drugs to ease their anxiety and depression.

Again, this is not to say that some of us do not suffer from chemical imbalances in the brain; many of us do, and for those, these psychiatric drugs are a godsend. But we must also be careful about what "problems" end up being "treated" by "solutions" which happen to be drug-based.

Thus we have evidence that children diagnosed as hyperactive responded positively to a lifestyle stripped of sugar, junk food, TV and video games. Imagine the immense reduction in profits if drugs, sugary snacks, junk food, TV and video games were no longer "consumed" by American children. *Cui bono* indeed.

The narratives that operate beneath the surface compress all of experience into a limited number of hammers; so when a nail resists, guess what happens? It gets pounded down. When you hold the hammer, that "solution" is "obvious."

Chapter Six: Propaganda and the Politics of Experience

Just as our "solutions" are shaped by how we frame "the problem," our understanding of our world is shaped by a "politics of experience" created by our cultural milieu, education, mass media and government.

As noted in the excerpt from R.D. Laing above, *the key feature of "the obvious" is its elusiveness.* Thus we don't consciously formulate the notion that what we buy and own defines our "true self;" that notion is like air, everywhere around us and thus not in our conscious awareness.

Our politics of experience is by definition not selected or consciously chosen; it is precisely the invisible assumptions we live by which are so unconscious that we cannot even recognize them as anything but "obvious" without great effort.

As Laing also described, the past's *politics of experience* is largely inaccessible to us for the same reason we cannot discern how unobvious our own "obvious" truly is: the assumptions were so deep and elusive that contemporary accounts never even mention them, and thus histories are only extrapolations of what was considered worthy of comment.

An excellent analogy to this problem can be found in the common Mississippi river barge of the 19th century. So common was this mode of river transport that no one bothered to fashion a drawing of one or count them. They literally vanished without a trace simply because they were too ubiquitous to elicit notice. Recently a few representatives have been exhumed from the mud; these forgotten artifacts are our only evidence of what was once unremarkable but vitally important.

Thus is it difficult for us to register how drastically our experience has changed over time. What seem "normal" and "obvious" to us—the constant bombardment of marketing, the financial stress of over-indebtedness, the insecurity of employment, the reliance on powerful psychotropic prescription medications to "get through life"-- are actually artifacts of an obviously destructive set of assumptions and values.

Individuals pursue their livelihoods in this peculiar state of unawareness in which they are unaware of what they are unaware of, and unaware of the consequences of the "obvious" incentives and assumptions that underpin their sense of identity and seemingly "conscious" choices.

As we explore the elusive qualities of our common "obvious" experience, we must differentiate between the mostly unconscious actions of most of us and the carefully plotted conscious actions of those seeking to influence our experience for specific gain.

For there is another class of citizenry for whom "the obvious" is an invitation to conscious manipulation.

For example: the first project of "the Powers That Be" is to deny the existence of The Powers That Be via a sustained propaganda campaign touting the great opportunities, justice and equality of our society and economy. The goal is to shape our interpretation of our experience into a pliable complacency which leaves the influence of the Plutocracy safely accepted as "natural" and thus unquestioned.

The "politics of experience" which operates at a subconscious level includes all the incentives and assumptions which form our worldview.

Here is another example: "the rugged individual" myth that is core to American society has many positive elements--for instance, the ideal of individual responsibility for one's life and actions--but it also works to mask political and financial overreach by the plutocracy/Powers That Be by cloaking large-scale movements of vast profits and power as the disconnected workings of unrelated individuals.

Recall how the "politics of experience" of the subprime mortgage meltdown was presented by the Mainstream Media as the fault of irresponsible subprime borrowers. Then, as the U.S. government funneled hundreds of billions of dollars in bailout funds to save the Plutocracy from losses, the full extent of the corruption, greed, recklessness and fraud within the investment banking/mortgage/finance complex was revealed.

The "politics" behind that interpretation was revealed as a clever masking of the true cause: a Plutocracy operating without regard for laws or regulations and unhindered by political oversight. Please read <u>Fiasco: The Inside Story of a Wall Street Trader</u> and <u>Greed, Fraud & Ignorance: A Subprime Insider's Look at the Mortgage Collapse</u> for fuller accounts of the chicanery, greed and blatant disregard for law and risk.

The Mainstream Media (MSM), a highly centralized, corporate-owned structure, is a key player in shaping the politics of experience.

One key concept/mechanism in the politics of experience that we need to understand is how simulacra are consciously presented as the "real thing" to protect the Elites' power and privileges.

Simulacrum is defined as "an insubstantial form or semblance of something."

Consider how the word "capitalism," with its powerful invocations of free markets, capital freely risked, transparency, entrepreneurship, etc., is constantly deployed to mask crony capitalism, which fundamentally undermines all the key elements of true capitalism.

Thus the crony capitalism on display when stupendous government bailouts are sunk into a handful of Plutocracy strongholds is masked by explanations that "we're doing this to save capitalism."

Capitalism does not require the State to borrow a trillion dollars and throw it into the coffers of the Plutocracy. What is being presented as "capitalism" by the Plutocracy and its MSM minions is in fact only a simulacrum of capitalism, a sham representation decorated with just enough shreds of resemblance to the real thing to fool the unwary.

Another key job of the mass media is to distract the populace from the political realities with endless entertainments, just as the Roman Empire provided the citizens of Rome with free bread and fully 175 days a year of free public entertainment.

So our national "politics of experience" serves three explicit goals:

1. Provide a superficially plausible simulacrum of justice, opportunity, equality, capitalism, good governance, etc., so the unskeptical/credulous will comply with the wishes of The Powers That Be and blame themselves (or a carefully designated "other group") for whatever is awry in their communities.

2. Offer up a cornucopia of compelling distractions via mindless "entertainments" and a broadcast media presenting a nonstop diet of "crimes, cops and docs" and a simulacrum of meaning and authenticity via social networks. (Please see my book Weblogs & New Media: Marketing in Crisis for more on the superficiality of social networking.)

This includes a politically potent entertainment of divisive finger-pointing and rancor which works to create superficially appealing "us and them" ideologies.

3. Construct a simulacrum of authenticity bound and defined by consuming, buying and presenting an attractive avatar in the media, i.e. a simulacrum of authority, "coolness" or celebrity which creates a sham *Infrastructure of Self* in a politics of experience dominated by hollow social networks, consuming/shopping and celebrity worship.

Since the key goal of the marketing/mass-media complex is to instill a pervasive sense of insecurity in each "consumer" then it is predictable that the consumer responds by constructing an *Infrastructure of Self* of various brands and symbols of identity (tattoos, certain brands of music, etc.) which is an absurd simulacrum of authentic identity.

An authentic identity can only be formed by actions and deeds based on coherent internal beliefs--what was once known as strength of character--and internal states (faith, rules of conduct, self-discipline, etc.) which are inaccessible to marketing.

The Web's potential for propagating knowledge, innovations and practical solutions via *self-organizing networks* is visible to all. (I mentioned self-organizing networks in Chapter One in describing how the Plutocracy was not a conspiracy or secret club as much as a group bound by the same self interests.) That the Web enables people to self-organize in ways which were simply not possible in a world limited to telephones, centralized print and broadcast media and physical travel is self-evident.

But such ephemeral self-organizing networks vary in utility and duration. Lacking the bonds created by meetings in the real world, most such collections have very limited lifespans and results.

Nonetheless the political leverage offered by networking technologies (the Web, SMS-mobile phone texting, wikis, blogs, etc.) is already so powerful that repressive central States quickly disrupt, jam or shut down these networks when their power is threatened by popular insurrection.

The profitability and reach of such networks has not been lost on the global media empires, which have quickly taken control of the commercial social networks.

In a peculiar distortion of friendship and shared interests, these corporate social networks are perceived by their members and owners alike as marketing vehicles: one ceaselessly promotes one's band or "brand" and uses one's page to organize marketing campaigns.

These facsimiles of community and friendship appeal to the population most vulnerable to the pervasive insecurity implicit in all marketing: teens. But as anyone who is a teen or knows teens knows, the inauthenticity and artifice of these social networks soon reveals itself and the teens slip into zombie membership, visible on corporate records but no longer engaged in the attempt to satisfy authentic longings with artificial constructs. (Yes, teens do use these networks to communicate with their real-world friends, but this is an extension of texting and the phone, a reflection of their existing network rather than some new community.)

If we examine social networks' politics of experience, we might conclude they are akin to South Seas Cargo Cults which sprouted up after World War Two ended and the nearly supernatural technology and wealth brought by the Americans to remote islands stopped coming.

In a painfully impossible hope of communicating with the vanished Aliens, Cargo Cult members painted rocks to look like radios and called for the ships to return. Social networks designed for profitable marketing are the equivalent of stone radios; true friendship and community cannot be "called forth" by avatars. The social and spiritual poverty of such counterfeit social structures starkly reveals the internal poverty of our collective experience.

Propaganda: Manipulating the Politics of Experience

Though "propaganda" does not fully cover all that I mean by the politics of experience (which includes assumptions which are largely subconscious and subliminal, i.e. "the obvious"), it is nonetheless important to understand how education actually makes one more vulnerable to carefully crafted propaganda. A classic text on the subject is Propaganda: The Formation of Men's Attitudes by Jacques Ellul.

The book Age of Propaganda: The Everyday Use and Abuse of Persuasion offers these principles of propaganda.

- Our data-processing capabilities are limited and so we are unable to critically review all the information we receive. As a result, we resort to so-called heuristics, simple rules for solving the problem. Heuristics are distilled from our previous experience in similar situations.
- Although relying on heuristics is a useful way of dealing with a decision-rich environment, basing our decisions primarily on heuristics is problematic. First, our heuristic cues may be false. Furthermore, a rule may be appropriate in certain situations but be misapplied in others. Another problem is that heuristics can be easily faked and manipulated. Knowledge of heuristics enables control our politics of experience.
- Shaping a favorable climate for the message is called pre-persuasion. If we establish the agenda and context then we shape the results. One technique is to use statements as axioms

such as "what everyone takes for granted" and "what everyone knows." Another is to attach black-or-white labels (positive or negative) to topics which cannot be easily disputed.

- Establish a "source credibility" of "experts" and/or attractive communicators to activate the audience's own self-persuasion.
- Create a simple message that focuses the audience's attention on the specific "problem" which will define their "solution."
- Mental shortcuts (heuristics) are most likely to be used when the audience is under time pressure and so overwhelmed with information that it becomes impossible to process it adequately. If the audience has little other knowledge or information, then they will base their decision on whatever heuristics come quickly to mind within the context already established in the pre-persuasion stage.
- Evoke an emotion that will effectively channel the audience toward the desired conclusion. Fear is often effective, as is guilt; feelings of obligation and indebtedness invoke reciprocity, so we acquiesce. Appeals to universal values we hold trigger the desire to agree, for we all want to be self-consistent.
- Recruit the audience to a small role in the larger "play." Individuals then feel committed to the Cause, setting the stage for their agreement to future actions.
- Define group parameters so that the audience feels "we are all on the same side." Once they feel "membership" then they will feel obliged to "follow the group."

Note how the concepts of "what's obvious" and "framing the problem defines the solution" seamlessly fit into propaganda's mechanisms.

An early pioneer of full-spectrum marketing/propaganda was Edward Bernays, who formalized his systemic approach in his book Propaganda. Bernays justified marketing as an essential element of democracy, even as he summarized his work as *engineering consent*: "The engineering of consent is the very essence of the democratic process, the freedom to persuade and suggest."

Given that a handful of Elite interests own the vast majority of mass media outlets, we conclude that what Bernays presented as the authentic "democratic process" was in fact merely a simulacrum, designed to lull the unwary into believing marketing is the core of a democracy. When we ask cui bono of his scheme, the answer is himself and his corporate/Elite clientele, not the citizenry.

Another essential text on the media's subjugation to marketing and Elites' interests is Manufacturing Consent: The Political Economy of the Mass Media.

Con Game: Full Spectrum Defense of the Status Quo

Let's begin by repeating this definition of simulacrum: an insubstantial form or semblance of something. The reason why someone would construct and deploy a simulacrum is (shall we risk this word?) obvious:

A simulacrum is used to mask or distort a reality that, once revealed, would cause the target audience to act in ways that would not serve the interests of those deploying the simulacrum.

The spectrum of simulacra runs from simple sidewalk confidence games to highly elaborate global propaganda campaigns.

In a simple con game, the facsimile of a "fair game of chance" (or "open market") is presented to the target audience to persuade them to put their money into what is the opposite of fair and open: a setup carefully rigged to transfer the target's wealth to the purveyor. In other words, the sham offers the illusion that the game/market might benefit the target, while the reality is the game has only one end-state: it only benefits the con-man/"house" at the expense of the targets/"marks."

For a context larger than the sidewalk con game, consider the stock market and its elaborate simulacrum of "open markets," "sound ratings" and "expert investment advice." The target audience--the tens of millions of citizens with money in retirement accounts and similar funds--have suffered stupendous losses in the past decade by trusting the ratings promising low risk and the "expert investment advisors" who counseled "stay fully invested for the long-term" and "buy on the dips."

Every one of these actions required the confidence and trust of the marks, and every one served the interests of Wall Street rather than the interests of the marks. Every one enabled Wall Street to maximize its profits and transaction fees using the marks' own money, and every one provided Wall Street with maximum opportunity to sell losing positions to the marks and transfer the marks' wealth to Wall Street.

Many of the exotic mortgages (during the housing bubble, these were known as "exotic;" now that reality has broken through the distortions, they're known as "toxic") were also first-order cons: a simulacrum of a legitimate mortgage was presented, along with simulacrum of supporting documents, in order to fleece the unwary mortgage holder/ home buyer into a transfer of wealth from the mark (both the holder of the mortgage and its eventual buyer in the global mortgage-backed securities market) to the con owners.

A persuasive facsimile offers many advantages, hence the great number of examples. The crooked construction contractor creates a plausible veneer of legitimacy--business cards, well-worn tools, perhaps even phony references provided by confederates--in order to persuade the homeowners to sign a contract and put money down for a job which will never be started.

The buyer of a counterfeit pharmaceutical, on the other hand, may be paying full price for a worthless medication; the replacement of a legitimate label and product with facsimiles offers huge rewards to the purveyors and nothing to the unwary buyer.

In each of these cases--the con, the seduction, the counterfeit--the potential gains far outweigh the cost of creating the simulacrum. This hugely imbalanced cost-benefit ratio explains the ubiquity and prevalence of cons, counterfeits and seductions in all cultures and eras.

The key defenses against simulacra are knowledge and experience. What Wall Street fears is not regulation (which can be watered down with subsequent lobbying) but a dearth of new marks willing to believe that Wall Street works to their benefit in a fair and open market.

But simulacra offer a much broader spectrum of deception beyond seductions, counterfeits and con games; the great power of the concept lies in its unification of a tremendous range of distortions, deceptions and obfuscations presented as authentic.

Within our analysis of the politics of experience, the fundamental mechanism simulacra provide is what I term *full spectrum defense of the Status Quo*. Such simulacra can be found in all time scales and settings, from marriages to nations.

Thus we find simulacrum not just in willfully conceived confidence games but in good-faith efforts to sustain or "reform" failing institutions.

A partner who is fundamentally indifferent to the marriage will consent to counseling, not just to appear willing to save the status quo, but perhaps to sustain their own self-image as one who "tried."

Managers and politicians will go through the process of "reforming" failed, corrupt institutions, not with the intention to deceive so much as to "play the part" they feel is demanded of them, even if they know the reforms are superficial and will not resolve structural problems.

Thus simulacra are designed and supported for a number of reasons beyond outright deception; their key feature is that they protect the self-interest of the participant and deflect challenges to that self-interest by deflecting criticism and any attempt to replace the status quo with something much less beneficial to the Power Elites.

Stated another way: as the Elites' interests diverge from those of the society as a whole, they construct elaborate simulacrums to win the society's compliance and complicity (that is, the self-aggrandizement of "I don't care, I got mine").

For example, though the actual contracts for the construction of a massive State project will have already been decided behind closed doors, a facsimile of "public participation" will be presented to foster the illusion that the process was transparent. A series of superficial "town hall" meetings is generally enough to mask the reality--an inside job all the way--with a soothing simulacrum of "democracy in action."

The same can be said of corporate annual meetings, show trials, and other simulacra of participation and fairness.

A key goal is the disruption of common-sense assessment and decisionmaking: what is called *the OODA loop:* (observation, orientation, decision, action.) If every step can be confused, obscured, distorted and deflected via disinformation, deceptive framing of the problem, etc., then the process of change itself will be crippled. This is a key goal of all State/Plutocracy: *by crippling all adaptation and transformation, the status quo is defended.*

The great irony, of course, is that every organism and system must adapt to changing circumstances if it is to survive, much less prosper; and so the rigid defense of the status quo against all challenges renders it brittle and increasingly unstable to unstoppable devolution/phase shift/collapse.

This irony is perhaps best reflected in the Elites' self-reinforcing mechanism of exempting themselves (both the private capital-Plutocracy and the State functionary/public union Elite) from the very market forces which impose adaptation, creative destruction and evolution. The irony is deepened by the Plutocracy and State's alleged worship of "the free market"--the very market each exempts itself from at every turn.

Thus our first step in parsing the politics of experience will always be to ask cui bono of all participants, and to dig through the simulacra (both the illusions of authenticity and the disruptions of OODA loops) to the underlying realities.

The second step will be to realize that complacency and complicity will always be self-serving for participants, even those with little to gain from supporting the status quo. Why is this so? Losing whatever crumbs one does receive by challenging the owners of the cake will always be riskier than remaining passively compliant and complicit.

Put another way: maintaining the security of the known (status quo) is inherently less risky than embarking on a new path because the outcome is unknown. While change might bring improvements, it might also result in catastrophe: losing even a very limited security would be far worse than passively accepting the status quo. We might even posit that risk aversion is a naturally selected trait.

Risk-aversion certainly explains why people stay in jobs and marriages they loathe--the risks of change are perceived as more dangerous than the suffering of staying put. This mechanism works on individual and societal levels alike.

If this is so, then transformation becomes inevitable only when the supposed security of the status quo gives way--when, for instance, the State becomes insolvent and its "security" is revealed as illusory. At that point it will become obvious that change is coming one way or the other and so the "low-risk" option of passive complicity is no longer available.

Thus open insurrection only occurs when the crumbs have been swept away, and there is no reason left to support the status quo. This is why the State's greatest power is distributing crumbs widely enough that few will be served by challenging the State's growing share of national income and its steadfast protection of the Power Elites. The ideal situation for the State (and thus the Plutocracy) is every family in the nation receives a payment from the State and abundant free entertainment (bread and circuses).

The State will only devolve when it can no longer fund this universal largesse or the swag is paid in a currency that has lost all value.

Chapter Seven: The Art of Survival, Taoism and the Warring States

In addition to the near-impossibility of long-term sustainability, *Splendid Isolation* has another drawback: an insurmountably intrinsic insecurity. (A version of this chapter was published on www.oftwominds.com in June, 2008.)

I'm not trying to be difficult, but I can't help cutting against the grain on topics like surviving the coming bad times when my experience runs counter to the standard received wisdom.

A common thread within most discussions of surviving bad times--especially really bad times--runs more or less like this: stockpile a bunch of canned/dried food and other valuable accoutrements of civilized life (generators, tools, canned goods, firearms, etc.) in a remote area far from urban centers, and then wait out the bad times, all the while protecting your stash with an array of weaponry and technology (night vision binoculars, etc.)

Now while I respect and admire the goal, I must respectfully disagree with just about every assumption behind this strategy. Once again, this isn't because I enjoy being ornery (please don't check on that with my wife) but because everything in this strategy runs counter to my own experience in rural, remote settings.

You see, when I was a young teen my family lived in the mountains. To the urban sophisticates who came up as tourists, we were "hicks" (or worse), and to us they were "flatlanders" (derisive snort).

Now the first thing you have to realize is that we know the flatlanders, but they don't know us. They come up to their cabin, and since we live here year round, we soon recognize their vehicles and know about how often they come up, what they look like, if they own a boat, how many in their family, and just about everything else which can be learned by simple observation.

The second thing you have to consider is that after school and chores (remember there are lots of kids who are too young to have a legal job, and many older teens with no jobs, which are scarce), boys and girls have a lot of time on their hands. We're not taking piano lessons and all that urban busywork. And while there are plenty of pudgy kids spending all afternoon or summer in front of the TV or videogame console, not every kid is like that.

So we're out riding around. On a scooter or motorcycle if we have one, (and if there's gasoline, of course), but if not then on bicycles, or we're hoofing it. Since we have time, and we're wandering all over this valley or mountain or plain, one way or another, then somebody will spot that trail of dust rising behind your pickup when you go to your remote hideaway. Or we'll run across the new road or driveway you cut, and wander up to see what's going on. Not when you're around, of course, but after you've gone back down to wherever you live. There's plenty of time; since you picked a remote spot, nobody's around.

Your hideaway isn't remote to us; this is our valley, mountain, desert, etc., all 20 miles of it, or what have you. We've hiked around all the peaks, because there's no reason not to and we have a lot of energy. Fences and gates are no big deal, (if you triple-padlock your gate, then we'll just climb over it) and any dirt road, no matter how rough, is just an open invitation to see what's up there. Remember, if you can drive to your hideaway, so can we. Even a small pickup truck can easily drive right through most gates (don't ask how, but I can assure you this is true). If nobody's around, we have all the time in the world to lift up or snip your barbed wire and sneak into your haven. Its remoteness makes it easy for us to poke around and explore without fear of being seen.

What flatlanders think of as remote, we think of as home. If you packed in everything on your back, and there was no road, then you'd have a very small hideaway--more a tent than a cabin. You'd think it was safely hidden, but we'd eventually find it anyway, because we wander all over this area, maybe hunting rabbits, or climbing rocks, or doing a little fishing if there are any creeks or lakes in the area. Or we'd spot the wisp of smoke rising from your fire one crisp morning, or hear your generator, and wonder who's up there. We don't need much of a reason to walk miles over rough country, or ride miles on our bikes.

When we were 13, my buddy J.E. and I tied sleeping bags and a few provisions on our bikes--mine was an old 3-speed, his a Schwinn 10-speed--and rode off into the next valley over bone-jarring dirt roads. We didn't have fancy bikes with shocks, and we certainly didn't have camp chairs, radios, big ice chests and all the other stuff people think is necessary to go camping; we had some matches, cans of beans and apple sauce and some smashed bread. (It didn't start out smashed, but the roads were rough. Note: if you ever suffer from constipation, I recommend beans and applesauce.)

We camped where others had camped before us, not in a

campground but just off the road in a pretty little meadow with a ring of fire-blackened rocks and a flat spot among the pine needles. We didn't have a tent, or air mattress, or any of those luxuries; but we had the smashed bread and the beans, and we made a little fire and ate and then went to sleep under the stars glittering in the dark sky.

There were a few bears in the area, but we weren't afraid; we didn't need a gun to feel safe. We weren't dumb enough to sleep with our food; if some bear wandered by and wanted the smashed bread, he could take it without bothering us. The only animal that could bother us was the human kind, and since few people walk 10 or more miles over rough ground in the heat and dust, then we'd hear their truck or motorbike approaching long before they ever spotted us.

We explored old mines and anything else we spotted, and then we rode home, a long loop over rutted, dusty roads. In summer, we took countless hikes over the mountainous wilderness behind his family cabin.

All of which is to say that the locals will know where your hideaway is because they have lots of time to poke around. Any road, no matter how rough, might as well be lit with neon lights which read, "Come on up and check this out!" If a teen doesn't spot your road, then somebody will: a county or utility employee out doing his/her job, a hunter, somebody. As I said, the only slim chance you have of being undetected is if you hump every item in your stash on your pack through trailess, roadless wilderness. But if you ever start a fire, or make much noise, then you're sending a beacon somebody will eventually notice.

The Taoists developed their philosophy during an extended era of turmoil known as the Warring States period of Chinese history.

One of their main principles runs something like this: if you're tall and stout and strong, then you'll call attention to yourself. And because you're rigid--that is, what looks like strength at first glance--then when the wind rises, it snaps you right in half.

If you're thin and ordinary and flexible, like a willow reed, then you'll bend in the wind, and nobody will notice you. You'll survive while the "strong" will be broken, either by unwanted attention or by being brittle.

Another thing to ponder is that the human animal is a much better predator than it is an elusive prey. Goats and wild turkeys and other animals have very keen senses of smell and hearing, and it's tough to get close without them smelling you or hearing you. They're well camouflaged, and since human sight is selected to detect movement and color, if they stay quite still we have a hard time spotting them.

In comparison, the human is a clumsy prey. It can't smell or hear very well, and it's large and not well camouflaged. Plus it's usually distracted and unaware of its surroundings. It doesn't take much to kill a human, either; a single-shot rifle and a single round of .22 long is plenty enough.

If the chips are down, and push comes to shove, then what we're discussing is a sort of war, isn't it? And if we're talking about war, then we should think about the principles laid down in The Art Of War by Sun Tzu quite some time ago.

The flatlander protecting his valuable depot is on the defensive, and anyone seeking to take it away (by negotiation, threat or force) is on the offensive. The defense can select the site for proximity to water, clear fields of fire, or what have you, but one or two defenders have numerous disadvantages. Perhaps most importantly, they need to sleep. Secondly, just about anyone who's plinked cans with a rifle and who's done a little hunting can sneak up and put away an unwary human. Unless you remain in an underground bunker 24/7, at some point you'll be vulnerable. And that's really not much of a life--especially when your food supplies finally run out, which they eventually will. Or you run out of water, or your sewage system overflows, or some other situation requires you to emerge.

So let's line it all up. Isn't a flatlander who piles up a high-value stash in a remote area with no neighbors within earshot or line of sight kind of like a big, tall brittle tree? All those chains and locks and barbed-wire fencing and bolted doors just shout out that the flatlander has something valuable inside that cabin/bunker/RV.

Now if he doesn't know any better, then the flatlander reckons his stash is safe. But what he's not realizing is that we know about his stash and his vehicle and whatever else can be observed. If some locals want that stash, then they'll wait for the flatlander to leave and then they'll tow the RV off or break into the cabin, or if it's small enough, disassemble it and haul it clean off. There's plenty of time, and nobody's around. That's pretty much the ideal setting for leisurely thieving: a high-value stash of goodies in a remote area accessible by road is just about perfect.

Let's say things have gotten bad, and the flatlander is burrowed into his cabin. Eventually some locals will come up to visit; in a truck if there's gas, on foot if there isn't. We won't be armed; we're not interested in taking the flatlander's life or goodies. We just want to know what kind of person he is. So maybe we'll ask to borrow his generator for a town dance, or tell him about the church food drive, or maybe ask if he's seen so-and-so around.

Now what's the flatlander going to do when several unarmed men approach? Gun them down? Once he's faced with unarmed guys, he can't very well conclude they're a threat and warn them off. But if he does, then we'll know he's just another selfish flatlander. He won't get any help later when he needs it; or it will be minimal and grudging. He just counted himself out.

Suppose some bad guys hear about the flatlander's hideaway and stash. All it takes to stalk any prey is patience and observation; and no matter how heavily armed the flatlander is, he'll become vulnerable at some point to a long-range shot. (Even body armor can't stop a headshot or a hit to the femoral artery in the thigh.) Maybe he stays indoors for 6 days, or even 60. But at some point the windmill breaks or the dog needs walking or what have you, and he emerges--and then he's vulnerable. The more visible and stringent the security, the more he's advertising the high value of his depot.

And of course guarding a high-value stash alone is problematic for the simple reason that humans need to sleep.

So creating a high-value horde in a remote setting is looking like just about the worst possible strategy in the sense that the flatlander has provided a huge incentive to theft/robbery and also provided a setting advantageous to the thief or hunter.

If someone were to ask this "hick" for a less risky survival strategy, I would suggest moving into town and start showing a little generosity rather than a lot of hoarding. If not in town, then on the edge of town, where you can be seen and heard.

I'd suggest attending church, if you've a mind to, even if your faith isn't as strong as others. Or join the Lions Club, Kiwanis or Rotary International, if you can get an invitation. I'd volunteer to help with the pancake breakfast fundraiser, and buy a couple tickets to other fundraisers in town. I'd mow the old lady's lawn next door for free, and pony up a dollar if the elderly gentleman in line ahead of me at the grocery store finds himself a dollar light on his purchase.

If I had a parcel outside town that was suitable for an orchard or other crop, I'd plant it, and spend plenty of time in the local hardware store and farm supply, asking questions and spreading a little money around the local merchants. I'd invite my neighbors into my little plain house so they could see I don't own diddly-squat except some second-hand furniture and a crappy old TV. And I'd leave my door open so anyone could see for themselves I've got very little worth taking.

I'd have my tools, of course; but they're scattered around and old and battered by use; they're not shiny and new and expensive-looking, and they're not stored all nice and clean in a box some thief could lift. They're hung on old nails, or in the closet, and in the shed; a thief would have to spend a lot of time searching the entire place, and with my neighbors looking out for me, the thief is short of the most important advantage he has, which is time.

If somebody's desperate enough or dumb enough to steal my old handsaw, I'll buy another old one at a local swap meet. (Since I own three anyway, it's unlikely anyone would steal all three because they're not kept together.)

My valuable things, like the water filter, are kept hidden amidst all the low-value junk I keep around to send the message that there's nothing worth looking at. The safest things to own are those which are visibly low-value, surrounded by lots of other mostly worthless stuff.

I'd claim a spot in the community garden, or hire a neighbor to till up my backyard, and I'd plant chard and beans and whatever else my neighbors suggested grew well locally. I'd give away most of what I grew, or barter it, or maybe sell some at the farmer's market. It wouldn't matter how little I had to sell, or how much I sold; what mattered was meeting other like-minded souls and swapping tips and edibles.

If I didn't have a practical skill, I'd devote myself to learning one. If anyone asked me, I'd suggest saw sharpening and beer-making. You're legally entitled to make beer for yourself, and a decent homebrew is always welcome by those who drink beer. It's tricky, and your first batches may blow up or go flat, but when you finally get a good batch you'll be very popular and well-appreciated if you're of the mind to share.

Saw-sharpening just takes patience and a simple jig; you don't need to learn a lot, like a craftsman, but you'll have a skill you can swap with craftsmen/women. As a carpenter, I need sharp saws, and while I can do it myself, I find it tedious and would rather rebuild your front porch handrail or a chicken coop in exchange for the saw-sharpening.

Pickles are always welcome in winter, or when rations get boring; the Germans and Japanese of old lived on black bread or brown rice and pickled vegetables, with an occasional piece of dried meat or fish. Learning how to pickle is a useful and easy-to-learn craft. There are many others. If you're a techie, then volunteer to keep the network up at the local school; do it for free, and do a good job. Show you care.

Because the best protection isn't owning 30 guns; it's having 30 people who care about you. Since those 30 have other people who care about them, you actually have 300 people who are looking out for each other, including you. The second best protection isn't a big stash of stuff others want to steal; it's sharing what you have and owning little of value. That's being flexible, and common, the very opposite of creating a big fat highly visible, high-value target and trying to defend it yourself in a remote setting.

I know this runs counter to just about everything that's being recommended by others, but if you're a "hick" like me, then you know it rings true. The flatlanders are scared because they're alone and isolated; we're not scared. We've endured bad times before, and we don't need much to get by. We're not saints, but we will reciprocate to those who extend their good spirit and generosity to the community in which they live and in which they produce something of value.

The best way to look out for Number One is to start looking out for Numbers Two through Twenty.

The alternative to a vulnerable Isolation and living-off-the-land mythology is to join The Remnant and lead by example, building a productive, sustainable future for one's family, community and nation.

Chapter Eight: The Remnant, the Pareto Principle and You

Leading by example can be a far more powerful force for positive change than is commonly understood. (A version of this chapter was originally published on www.oftwominds.com on June 25, 2008.)

Oftwominds.com contributor U. Doran sent in a link to this essay which was published in the depths (Year 7) of the Great Depression: *Isaiah's Job* by Albert Jay Nock (from *The Atlantic Monthly*, 1936)

> In the year of Uzziah's death, the Lord commissioned the prophet (Isaiah) to go out and warn the people of the wrath to come. "Tell them what a worthless lot they are." He said, "Tell them what is wrong, and why and what is going to happen unless they have a change of heart and straighten up. Don't mince matters. Make it clear that they are positively down to their last chance. Give it to them good and strong and keep on giving it to them."
>
> "I suppose I ought to tell you," He added, "that it won't do any good. The official class and their intelligentsia will turn up their noses at you and the masses will not even listen. They will all keep on in their own ways until they carry everything down to destruction, and you will probably be lucky if you get out with your life."
>
> Isaiah had been very willing to take on the job — in fact, he had asked for it — but the prospect put a new face on the situation. It raised the obvious question: Why, if all that were so — if the enterprise were to be a failure from the start — was there any sense in starting it?
>
> "Ah," the Lord said, "you do not get the point. There is a Remnant there that you know nothing about. They are obscure, unorganized, inarticulate, each one rubbing along as best he can. They need to be encouraged and braced up because when everything has gone completely to the dogs, they are the ones who will come back and build up a new society; and meanwhile, your preaching will reassure them and keep them hanging on. Your job is to take care of the Remnant, so be off now and set about it."

Let's follow up on this notion of "Remnant" by invoking the Pareto Principle.

If the parameters in the Pareto distribution are suitably chosen, then one would have not only 80% of effects coming from 20% of causes, but also 80% of that top 80% of effects coming from 20% of that top 20% of causes, and so on (80% of 80% is 64%; 20% of 20% is 4%, so this implies a "64-4 law").

This suggests that a mere 4% of the 300 million Americans could influence 192 million of their fellow citizens. Since children and the very elderly generally wield less influence than those adults of working and child-bearing age, let's subtract the 60 million Americans under 14 years of age and the 18 million over 75 years of age (*Annual Estimates of the Population by Sex and Five-Year Age Groups for the United States: April 1, 2000 to July 1, 2007*, U.S. Census Bureau).

That leaves about 220 million Americans between 14 and 75 years of age. 4% of that number is 8.8 million. So the critical number for the Remnant in the U.S. appears to be about 9 million people.

When 9 million people start leading (4%), then 140 million (64%) will follow. Once those 150 million are moving in the same direction, then they will collectively be an irresistible force for positive change.

As the essay so brilliantly describes, members of the Remnant are not on the pulpit or writing for the Mainstream Media; they are unpublicized, unnoticed, perhaps viewed as outsiders by those around them, perhaps not. But their influence is generated by action and example, not by preaching, pontificating or cajoling.

Given the government's abysmal non-response to the growing financial and energy crises, then I conclude the 9 million will have to lead government, not vice versa.

Note that the Remnant is not engaged in any one pursuit; smart people are just doing what they think is right and good, which includes being skeptical of the received "wisdom" of the media's pronouncements, trying to avoid the financial vortex which is pulling down the non-elites living lighter, cheaper, better lifestyles away from the stomping masses of the Consumption Is Our True God mainstream, working to improve the soil of a patch of earth, and a thousand other projects and interests.

If anything characterizes the Remnant, it is skepticism, a disdain for aggrandizement, and an awareness that doing with less is actually a happier, more fulfilling life than Always Chasing More in the Public Eye.

Though The Remnant works locally, it is simultaneously acting on a national level—not in an organized fashion, but in a Remnant fashion, by example and in transparent self-organized networks.

Chapter Nine: The Structure of Happiness

Now that the credit/debt-based simulacrum of prosperity has imploded, so too has the consumption-fantasy simulacrum of happiness.

Just as a capitalism founded on production and risk/return has been undermined by crony-capitalism and governance has been replaced by self-aggrandizement, looting and pandering, so too has an experience-based understanding of happiness been reduced to a threadbare simulacrum of shopping, buying, consuming and owning.

If happiness requires a full-employment, credit-dependent, high-cost, fossil-fuel dependent, consumption-based economy that is no longer sustainable, then clearly there will be a corresponding increase in unhappiness as the U.S. economy devolves.

Rather than throw trillions of dollars away in a futile attempt to rekindle a bubble/credit/crony capitalism which has run its course, perhaps it would be wiser (as well as much cheaper) to unburden ourselves of this equally doomed definition of happiness in favor of a sustainable, healthier understanding of well-being: what I term *full spectrum prosperity*.

Full spectrum prosperity is simply the recognition that "real wealth" cannot be measured by one's possessions but by health (the only irreplaceable wealth), access to the FEW essentials (food, energy and water), meaningful skills deployed in meaningful work and a network of people who care about your well-being. Such mutual concern is founded on reciprocity, i.e. that you actively contribute to the well-being of those who contribute to your well-being.

Lip service is of course paid to such non-quantifiable measures of well-being, but the admiration and respect of the status quo, including many churches, is nonetheless reserved for the financially "successful." Those who aren't wealthy are marginalized in a Darwinian metric derived entirely from financial statistics.

This is not accidental. Water and food in their natural forms simply aren't profitable, and a low-energy intensive lifestyle is equally devoid of profit potential.

If we state that the most valuable possession one can have is personal integrity, this is essentially meaningless in financial terms and therefore it is valueless in the current consumerist frame of reference.

Our integrated understanding is that unprofitable concepts,

experiences and objects are *derealized* in favor of services and goods which can be sold at enormous profit via pervasive mass media marketing.

Thus personal integrity is derealized and tap water is filtered and sold at a stupendous premium in plastic bottles with a brand attached. Real food plucked from the earth is derealized in favor of packaged food loaded with an engineered mix of salt, sugar and fat that is carefully designed to trigger the "reward" centers of the human brain even as it causes chronic disease and deranges the mind.

The goal of the mass marketing/propaganda system is to create what I term an *imaginary causal connection* between an internal state of satiation/satisfaction (in the adolescent framework the system has established as "obvious," this passes for "happiness") and the purchase of profitable goods and services.

The imaginary/fantasy character of advertising/marketing is well-known but less well known is the divergence between the initial causal connection--buying this brand of brandy causes the consumer to experience a sense of coveted elitism sorely lacking in the rest of his/her life--and the quick degradation of this initial reaction into the background insecurity of ennui (boredom)/dissatisfaction/deprivation/pain.

The sad irony is that the marketing/consumerist version of happiness is actually only a simulacrum of true happiness.

The "consumer" experiences happiness only for the fleeting moments of selection and purchase. The inner poverty of this simulacrum remains, gnawing away at whatever fulfillment is left to the incurably insecure "consumer."

This simulacrum of happiness has been distilled down by the marketing/advertising complex to a simplistic, superficial formula:

1. You are a consumer

2. A consumer's worth is measured externally by what is owned, worn, displayed, and by what high-status markers are certified by authority (diploma, elite membership, etc.) or the mass media (desirable avatar, high profile, etc.)

3. Self-worth results from the acquisition of goods and external markers

4. The internal state of consuming/owning scarcity-valued goods and high-status markers is happiness

What is left unspoken is the motivation for this formula:

5. The purpose of this formula is to profitably sell the insecure consumer an unnecessary good or marker which has an entirely imaginary connection to self-worth and happiness.

Being social mammals, humans' reproductive success depends to some degree on the level of status, power and material wealth each individual reaches; thus some 8% of the men in a wide swath of Asia carry genes which trace back to the extraordinarily prolific conqueror Genghis Khan.

But to equate high social status with happiness is to confuse two complex issues: higher status may well provide more access to material sources of well-being, but happiness--a state of mind, an understanding, a practice and a process--cannot be reduced to material ownership.

Indeed, numerous studies of the multi-faceted inner sensation we call happiness (which I would term well-being) conclude that the sources of happiness are largely internal and relationship-based rather than material or status-based. Common sense suggests that the security offered by wealth and income boosts well-being, but studies find additional wealth provides diminishing returns. Beyond a certain relatively low level, additional wealth in any form (cash, goods, travel, etc.) offers little improvement in well-being.

Factors often listed as sources of well-being include: Meaningful work, recreation, love, friendship and worship.

We might ask: since shopping did not make the list, how did the pursuit of happiness shrivel to the pursuit of goods and services?

The answer is self-evident: a secure individual identity does not require status or limitless externalities, and thus it does not offer many opportunities to sell unneeded goods and services at a profit.

The first project of the marketing/advertising system is to break down internally produced self-worth and identity and replace it with a permanent insecurity.

Convince the target audience that their worth is not internally sourced but totally dependent on externalities, and you create a fundamental insecurity: one can never have enough external goods or markers to establish enduring inner security.

A new fad or status marker will soon be introduced, driving down the value of whatever you own and thus your own "value" will plummet. Gratitude is impossible when there is never enough.

In a peculiar dynamic, the derealization of inner security--that is, of *an independently constructed sense of self*--by relentless marketing has sparked the emergence of a simulacrum of identity and self-worth: the so-called self-esteem industry.

Such is the perfection of the marketing/advertising system's induced insecurity that the connection between relentless marketing and our culture's pervasive sense of inner worthlessness is never made.

Rather than identify the root cause--the marketing/advertising complex--the self-esteem industry focuses on the symptoms, which it attempts to ameliorate with simplistic "feel-good" slogans ("you can be anything you want!", etc.), a counterproductive reduction in standards and a profoundly distorting goal of eliminating all metrics which might introduce a sense of diminished self-worth.

Just as the marketing complex purposefully confuses happiness with consumption (and indeed, citizen with consumer), so too does the self-esteem industry confuse external metrics and slogans with inner security and well-being.

Even some elements of organized religion have accepted the consumerist framework. In a troubling distortion of the Bible's edict that "It is easier for a camel to go through the eye of a needle than for a rich man to enter into the kingdom of God," some churchgoers have come to confuse wealth acquisition with spiritual attainment.

The Declaration of Independence's "pursuit of happiness"--implicitly a structured process, a journey toward a goal--has been replaced with an illusory and ultimately cruelly misleading end-state: happiness has been reduced from a structured journey (with inevitable setbacks) to the fleeting euphoria of a new purchase/acquisition.

An experience-based understanding of happiness is ontologically structured around the experiences of well-being, warmth and satisfaction offered by true friendship, accomplishment, generosity, romantic and spiritual love and the humility of worship. The acquisition of externalities and superficial markers has no place in this understanding.

In a parallel fashion, an *independently constructed sense of self*-- what we term an individual's identity--grows from humility, accountability, responsibility, self-knowledge, and the strength of personal integrity, not from an illusory simulacrum of identity conjured by pronouncements ("I am a member of...") and possessions.

Indeed, all that is truly valuable in one's self and identity can never be taken away or even diminished: integrity, experience, self-knowledge and humility.

Rather than accept the derealizing, dehumanizing reduction to passive consumer, the individual seeking internal and external liberation must renounce the impoverishment of "consumer" and embrace the power of a citizen's independently constructed sense of self.

One key feature of the marketing/advertising derealization is the erosion of adulthood in favor of a facsimile of adulthood: *permanent adolescence.*

The very traits needed to negotiate adulthood--an awareness of being tricked/manipulated/cheated, an awareness that life is a series of trade-offs in which one desire is sacrificed to support another deemed more important, the ability to put aside short-term impulses to meet long-term goals, the acceptance of responsibility and "no excuses/no blaming others for my own faults" accountability, etc.--are derealized in favor of an easily malleable adolescent worldview of impulse, denial of accountability, malleable (and thus worthless) integrity, immediate gratification of appetites, escape from boredom and an obsessively insecure monitoring of one's peers for approval.

The adolescent is the perfect marketing target: insecure, focused on gaining approval via external props and cues, easily distracted and bored, powerfully stimulated by "newness" (a key feature of marketing exploitation), drawn to "tribes" of prescribed behavior and identity, fearful of consequences and thus attracted to denial and assigning blame to others, and prone to powerful sensory surges triggered by sexual and physical signals (taste, scent, etc.).

The ideal adolescent can barely restrain his/her impulses and emotions and is ever ready to indulge whims and desires. He/she is intensely insecure and doesn't trust his/her own experience but instead seeks the approval of peers or peer tribes via marketable clothing or other externals, suppressing his/her own inner life and experiences lest they conflict with the security offered by conformity. Regardless of the apparent marginality of the tribe he/she belongs to, the conformity is equally intense, marketable and unthreatening to the State and the Plutocracy.

The more the "consumer" internalizes these positive cues for adolescence, the more they experience their own alienation as their own fault; given that the very adulthood skills they would need to break free of the trap have been eroded/derided by marketing, they find their inability to feel what they're supposed to be feeling ("happy") only drives them further into compulsive, self-destructive behaviors (the primordial "eating a quart of ice cream in the bathtub" experience, cutting oneself, sexual/drug excesses, etc.).

The very shallowness of this ubiquitously marketed adolescent worldview insures the participating consumer will feel unfulfilled and insecure after the brief high of consumption wears off. Unable to cross the chasm to their own experience, they turn with increasing desperation to marketed escapes and distractions for relief.

The Debt-Serf Consumerist Connection

Debt is slavery of the free. Publilius Syrus, Rome, 1st Century B.C.E.

Debt-serfdom--that is, the funneling of the lion's share of household income to debt service--is intimately connected to the false ideology of consumerism. Here is the key concept: **the products purchased all have an end value of zero while the debt lives on.** After the initial thrill of purchase--somewhat like an addict's initial euphoria—the purchase quickly falls to zero value even as the interest due continues on.

Every purchase other than land, gold, silver, a well-built house and a working system of energy production falls to near-zero value. A well-made and maintained vehicle may last 20 years, but the value will fall precipitously as it ages.

Unfortunately, many consumer goods are simulacrum of former products. Thus a piece of furniture which was once crafted of real wood and thus built to last hundreds of years is now fabricated of wood chips, glue and a paper-thin veneer which offers the facsimile of wood grain. This faux furniture will break apart within a few years (or even months), meaning that the credit card debt will outlast the furniture.

This connection is important, as the financial Elite profits immensely from high-interest consumer credit.

The free are thus enslaved via consumerist debt.

When Consumerist Gods Fail

It is important to recall the context of the current Depression: the U.S. has consumed trillions of dollars of goods and commodities in exchange for rapidly depreciating paper. Once credit/debt cannot be created exponentially, then consumption will fall in line with surplus production.

The marketing complex will still be flooding every nook and cranny of the nation and its media with messages to consume, but if few have surplus money and credit then it follows that few will have the means to buy, regardless of the persuasiveness of the millions of messages.

Thus it is not that the false god of consumerism will be toppled but that it will be abandoned--in many cases, most sorrowfully--by believers and adherents who no longer possess the surplus cash to offer the consumerist god.

The key factor in a consumerist-based identity is that someone profits by selling you an identity, character and sheen of status.

The idea that what you wear, drive, tattoo yourself with, load on your iPod, etc. has zero bearing on anything meaningful about who you are and what you value is subversive sacrilege of the highest order.

If "my stuff" is no longer "me," then who and what am I? And indeed, what can I sell you if all you really need to be "yourself" and happy is friends, minimal shelter, unprocessed food, homemade music, a library and an Internet connection and spiritual communion/worship? How much profit can I make selling you a used guitar, a DSL connection and a bag of carrots?

It boils down to this: when you run out of money, you switch religions from Consumerism to one of the good old spiritual standbys.

The known sources of happiness require little to no consumption:

1. health
2. friends
3. free time to pursue interests
4. spiritual communion/worship
5. exercise/sports/play
6. gardening
7. meaningful work (unpaid qualifies)

The experience of well-being has been so derealized that the sense of deprivation experienced at the loss of fine dining, Caribbean cruises, season tickets to the games, etc. is itself suspect.

We might even speculate that the experience of genuine happiness and well-being has largely been forgotten, or perhaps is an unknown sensation to media-numbed "consumers."

Since sustaining the simulacrum of consumerist "happiness" will cause much misery as the consumerist economy slides to oblivion, we might profitably ask if the happier choice wouldn't be to jettison the entire artifice of consumerist "happiness." Upon reflection, it was never real happiness after all; it was only a means to reap immense profits.

Dependency, Entitlement, Resentment and the State

There are few conditions more debilitating than dependency. Dependency leaches away self-confidence and leaves insecurity, self-loathing and a self-destructive resentment in its place.

There are two great ironies in Rise of the State (both Marxist and Neoliberal Capitalist) in the past century. One is that the State's nurturing of entitlements (and thus dependency) has been "sold" to the citizenry as "providing security" but as noted elsewhere, it has effectively bought the citizenry's silent complicity in the Plutocracy/State's expanding dominance of the nation's assets and income.

The second irony that rather than provide security, this dependence has actually crippled the citizenry by fostering an amoral "game the system" mentality in which integrity is sacrificed for a perversely rewarding worship of victimhood. Those who sacrifice truth and integrity to file bogus claims are rewarded while those who tell the unadorned truth--such as, yes, I can still work in some capacity--are punished.

Those exaggerating their victim status--a form of outright fraud which has become not just commonplace but acceptable--game the system to the disadvantage of the self-reliant and responsible.

These perverse incentives and feedbacks have created a system in which firefighters claim a heart murmur (a very common and notably benign condition--I have one) as a work-relayed "disability" which then allows their already outsized pensions to flow to them tax-free.

As with finance and politics, the devolution of honesty and integrity has been shunted from public discourse; it would be "rude," insensitive" or "judgmental" to simply state that the firefighters claiming a heart murmur as a work-related injury are misrepresenting the truth. No one dares demand the truth lest their own claim to entitlement be rejected out of spite by those who have sold their personal integrity for State swag.

With integrity rendered not just worthless but a liability and dependency ascendant, then citizens are effectively encouraged by these State dependency incentives to file "stress claims" and "crazy money" (SSI, disability paid out of the Social Security system) and dozens of other frauds.

Indeed, "disability" is now a major drain on the economy at large, though the reality is the vast majority of people claiming disability could still be productive in some fashion. Yes, a small percentage of the populace is truly incapable of being productive--the quadriplegic, the severely psychotic, etc. But there are many "jobs" which even the severely disabled could perform; the simple but highly valuable service of providing "eyes on the street" could be performed by many currently classified as disabled/unable to work.

The key problem with State-encouraged dependency is the internal damage done to what I term *internally derived security*, the confidence of those who have learned to trust their own intuition/judgment, their own ability to learn and adapt and their own inner/spiritual resilience. Come what may, these people have confidence in themselves and their beliefs. They have the experience to back up their confidence--experience built on mistakes, errors and failures.

In the pillowy soft embrace of a perniciously destructive dependence on the State, the concept of *radical self-reliance* sounds harsh and "judgmental," as if dependency has created such a fragility of spirit and intellect that we cannot even bear to hear that we are now crippled by dependency. As with all derealizations and illusions, silence does not make the reality go away; a forbidden topic merely worms deeper into the soul and wreaks ever-greater damage to those seeking to hide it.

It is an irony of human nature that dependency offers the illusion of freedom--freedom from want and freedom of purpose. Yet the exact opposite is true: for in a Devil's Pact, the acceptance of dependency requires the sacrifice of real security--that you can take care of yourself, think for yourself and learn/adapt/pick yourself up on your own.

Ironically, self-reliance is freedom and dependence is a pernicious form of servitude.

Dependency also demands the sacrifice of self-worth and independence. Fearful of his/her own weakness (confirmed by the dependency) and thus fearful of losing the zero-sum game of divvying up the State's tax revenue, the dependent harbors resentment against everyone: other competitors drawing swag from the State, the State for being miserly, critics who question the lies, obfuscation and fraud at the heart of the system and even those who are paying the taxes which fund the entitlements.

The entitlement mindset is equally destructive, feeding multiple resentments and insecurities; the mind of the entitled dependent is filled with justifications, rationalizations, explanations and excuses for why they "deserve" not just the "right" to the State's largesse but the further "right" to their own hostility and resentments.

The resentful dependent (on the State or any other entity) is not a fulfilled person-- ontologically, dependence breeds resentment and crumbles inner strengths and thus it is incapable of fostering fulfillment or happiness.

Self-reliance--what I term radical self-reliance to differentiate it from the simulacrum of "self-reliance" used to mask various levels of dependency--flows from the inner sources of security: experience, belief in oneself and a sturdy belief in the goodness and importance of positive actions, on one's own behalf and just as importantly, on behalf of others.

The voices which rise in strident defense of entitlements are wasting their energy, for the State and its entitlements are doomed to insolvency, and nothing will stop that devolution and collapse.

Thus the only question is what we as a society will do with ourselves once we are thrown back on our own resources by the crumbling of the State's dependency machinery. Just as the servant/serf who feared the bankruptcy of his Master on the principle that the unknown is more unsettling than servitude, the citizenry may awaken in the financial ruins of the State and discover that illusions of security were just that, and that freedom requires self-reliance--and self-reliance requires sustained, well-thought out but flexible action toward limited, carefully selected goals.

Perhaps that sums up life, liberty and the pursuit of happiness.

The Structure of Happiness

Let us revisit a key concept:
This process of bridging the widening gap between what we experience and what we're being told we should be experiencing via the substitution of simulacrum for authentic structures is central to this entire analysis.

In other words: when we have lost the possibility of indulging the marketing system's fantasy of endless consumption of needless goods and services, instead of feeling the loss, deprivation and gnawing sense of insecurity/emptiness we are supposed to experience, we might well feel an unexpected but deeply genuine relief that the burdens of constant consumption have been lifted from our sagging shoulders.

It won't be surprising that an analysis which refers so often to the "politics of experience" seeks to illuminate the darkest corner of the consumerist theology: that the politics of experience deep within an apparently superficial consumerism is a form of servitude, and that the collapse of that theology is liberation.

That is, we do not experience happiness or fulfillment in a vacuum; it is difficult to pursue happiness in a political structure of randomized violence, suppression of free expression, insecure private property rights, theft by other means and centralized, ubiquitous propaganda that is dominated by an over-reaching State and its Plutocratic overlords.

Thus if we consider the Founding Fathers' phrase "pursuit of happiness" closely, we find not only that it implies a personal pathway of goals, progress, setbacks and discipline rather than a static end-state but also a political environment in which the individual pursuit of happiness is not just possible but encouraged rather than suppressed.

Perhaps the first step to such an understanding of an authentic "pursuit of happiness" is to recognize the consumerist theology of insatiable acquisition as a perverse and destructive simulacrum of genuine happiness.

Chapter Ten: The Process of Internal Transformation

By definition, internal transformation means our understanding and worldview have changed even as the external world remains unchanged.

By changing our internal expectations, we eliminate one source of misery and internal strife.

Studies have revealed a common-sense correlation between happiness and expectations: those (usually low-income) with low expectations which can actually be met are significantly happier than those with high expectations which cannot be met. Thus part of the process of moving from unhappiness, hostility, grief and loss to acceptance, hope and a positive view of life is to reconcile unrealistic internalized (often manufactured by the mass media) expectations with what life actually offers.

A classic example of the causal nature of expectations originated in Hong Kong a few years ago. Immigrant maids who worked long hours six days a week for wealthy Hong Kong households were found to be much happier than their employers, who often suffered from depression, anxiety and even thoughts of suicide. By the usual material measures of "success and happiness," the outcome should have been reversed.

But while the bourgeois Hong Kong residents internalized expectations for wealth, success and recognition which were impractical or impossible to meet, the maids were buoyed by the meaning of the labor--supporting their families back home in the Philippines--and by their one day of socializing with other immigrant workers.

This essential transformation of expectations is made all the more difficult by the consumerist marketing ethos described earlier which generates insecurity, dissatisfaction and unrealistic externally-dependent expectations as key motivators for buying unneeded goods and services (and thus generating profits).

An entire constellation of complex emotions may be triggered by a devolution in financial wealth and loss of home and livelihood: anger, resentment, grieving, confusion, and even betrayal. The thinking may follow this line: I did what was expected of me, I played by the rules, I worked hard, and now my life is a shambles. This isn't right, it's not fair.

When the credit-dependent path of perversely dissatisfying "material happiness" comes to an end, many who believed in the system may well feel betrayal as well as loss. These emotions may parallel those felt by people who have been intimately betrayed by loved ones or betrayed by business/financial partners. They may feel they "did their part" and as such they don't deserve this harsh fate.

The entitlement mindset that we are each "owed" a pension, healthcare, housing, a livelihood, etc., by the Savior State also feeds a self-defeating resentment and sense of betrayal.

The underlying assumption was that the exponential-credit/bubble economy was supposed to "work" in some enduring fashion: higher debt was supposed to enable a "nicer" lifestyle, rising housing values were supposed to effortlessly fund a permanent increase of material improvements, and so on. The collapse of security and assets/equity may feel like a betrayal, and all those who feel betrayed by their own self-destructive actions will feel a great temptation to blame someone other than themselves.

Ironically, the very forces which rigged the game and manufactured the politics of experience which fostered the delusions of grandeur (wealth without saving or sacrifice, etc.) are rarely identified as responsible by the average middle class citizen, who has been trained to "accept responsibility" rather than probe abstract structural forces.

Thus the person experiencing resentment, betrayal, grief, loss and anger may well blame something other than the two actual causes: their own actions and choices (i.e. embracing the delusion of exponential credit expansion and ephemeral wealth as real) and the marketing/media system which profited from their embrace of delusion.

The process of accepting personal responsibility for one's actions and seeing the system for what it truly is beneath the superficial simulacrum is a painful one for all of us. But placing personal integrity above all else is immensely freeing.

Many who undergo this transformation of understanding describe the feeling as liberating, as if a great burden had been lifted from their shoulders. All that they once thought so important--the private school, the expansive house, the nameplate vehicle, the title, degree or corner office, the seasons tickets to the ball game, and so on--are revealed as unimportant compared to health, family, friends, acting in good faith and with complete individual integrity, true productivity, simple food and simple pleasures.

This transformation eventually extends from accepting responsibility for one's own health, retirement, livelihood and spiritual attainment to a realization that each citizen is also responsible for the larger community tasks of education, governance and security. Once the Savior State collapses into insolvency, this larger responsibility of each citizen will become clear to all.

This transformation is thus not just accepting lower expectations; it also requires consciously chosen positive action. The following quote by Nikola Tesla, submitted by oftwominds.com reader Kenneth R., neatly encapsulates this understanding:

"Every effort under compulsion demands a sacrifice of life energy."

We might also add this quote from Eric Hoffer: *"We lie the loudest when we lie to ourselves."*

Hoffer was one of the first thinkers to grasp how mass movements (religious and political alike) acted as a substitute for self-worth; this is the basis of their tremendous appeal to people who feel lost, adrift, without hope, etc. Hoffer clearly identified the Devil's Pact nature of mass movements: even as they gave the "believers" a newfound, heady sense of purpose and empowerment, they enabled destructive fanaticism and took away the individual's ability to think or judge for himself. This Devil's Pact inevitably leads to fascism, authoritarianism, loss of democracy and national self-destruction.

From one perspective, the entire "religion" of credit-dependent, media-driven consumerism which is the "engine of the U.S. economy" is just such a destructive mass movement; individual critical thinking and engagement in the real world are diverted and diminished in order to maximize the Plutocracy/State's profit and power.

Put another way: the distraction and self-destruction of the citizenry serves the financial-banking Plutocracy and the State quite admirably.

The process of internal transformation is essentially one of illusion, artifice and self-serving denial being replaced by truth, acceptance and integrity.

Chapter Eleven: The Principles of Systemic Response

It is an odd trait of both markets and human beings that by the time collapse is unfolding, it is too late to change the momentum or set up alternative plans. The Chinese have a proverb that expresses this very concisely: "When you're thirsty, it's too late to dig a well."

Essentially we face two basic choices: either complacently habituate to devolution and fatalistically accept the dire consequences of collapse, or take goal-directed actions which have a high probability of improving the odds that the Great Transformation will be positive--for us, for our communities and for our nation.

We come now to the heart of our integrated understanding and the responses that are most likely to foster prosperity and security.

Let's establish these contexts:

- The responses are built on principles, not "one size fits all" solutions. There are no "one size fits all" fixes to the many challenges we face as individuals/households, communities and as a nation. Solutions will be specific to individuals and communities and voluntarily chosen, not imposed.
- The Internet is integral to the transparency and exchange of ideas that will enable positive responses.
- Hybrid models of work, collaboration, capital, production and trade will replace highly centralized, "factory" hierarchical models in many situations.
- Solutions and responses are dynamically evolving in response to changing circumstances and feedbacks. Thus there is no one investment strategy which will maintain purchasing power in all circumstances. Flexibility, adaptability and acceptance of failure as part of the process are key to successfully navigating the dynamic era ahead. *"Success consists of going from failure to failure without loss of enthusiasm."* (Winston Churchill)
- Since *"There is no security on this earth, there is only opportunity"* (Douglas MacArthur), contingency planning—having a "Plan B"—is essential in every situation.

The ultimate context of our integrated understanding is that the world must use the remaining extractable reserves of fossil fuels to construct an alternative energy system that does not rely on cheap, abundant fossil fuels. The cost of such a global system is unknown, but let's start with $100 trillion or roughly three years of global GDP as an estimate.

As noted in the full *Survival+* text, wealth is simply stored energy. Without energy, there is no wealth. Virtually all of what we consider wealth is merely a reflection or consequence of cheap, abundant oil.

If humanity foolishly consumes the last of its planetary "gift" of easily extractable oil, coal and natural gas on vacations, suburban lifestyles and other non-productive uses, then when fossil fuels enter the final depletion stage there won't be enough left to construct a sustainable energy system.

We have discussed how the middle class is being squeezed to extinction and how the concentration of power and capital has created institutional and systemic vulnerability. We have also described the insurmountable barriers to reforms and thus established that devolution and insolvency are the inevitable end-state of the current system.

Let us now turn to The Principles of Systemic Response that have a high probability of making the Transformation positive.

These principles are scale-invariant, meaning that they apply equally to individuals, households, enterprises, communities and nation-States.

1. Engagement. Democracy is a feedback loop that requires active engagement. Democracy and the liberties it protects cannot be sustained by any "launch and forget" mechanisms. Setting up a regulatory system does not mean no further input is necessary; concentrations of capital and power will eventually capture or co-opt any State structure. That is the nature of Elites and the nature of State bureaucracies.

The majority of citizens are disengaged from participatory democracy. Barely 40% can rouse themselves to vote, never mind serve on committees, lobby local government, contact their representatives, etc. If a people get the government they deserve, then disengagement deserves devolution and collapse.

It is insightful to understand democracy as a series of feedback loops. The Elites will always have access to the State decisionmakers-- this is a feedback loop. As their power becomes more concentrated, then they can purchase ever more influence over the State and thus funnel an ever-larger share of the national income into their accounts. This is a positive feedback loop.

The feedback from the citizens is weak to non-existent and thus it has to date offered little resistance to the positive feedbacks of the Elites and State. Even though introducing (or re-introducing) citizen feedback seems to have no effect, the Pareto Principle suggests that a mere 4% of the citizenry can greatly influence 64%.

As the interests of the Elite and State have diverged from the common interest, a *profound political disunity* has emerged. As we have seen from the example of Rome, the Elites will fight to maintain the status quo even as the Empire collapses around them. No estate, no matter how well-defended, can escape the consequences of devolution.

This disunity/disharmony is the inevitable result of Elite/State over-reach. The ultimate goal of an engaged citizenry is not to "save" the self-destructive State and Elites from the consequences of their over-reach, but to establish the foundation of what I term *The New State* which can only arise from the ashes of the failed Savior State. This will require transparency and robust feedback loops from the citizenry to the State.

If the citizenry are not already engaged, then there will be no foundation for a New State to emerge.

Advocacy--that is, demanding a larger slice of State spoils--is not engagement, it is lobbying. If we begin by asking *cui bono*, then the difference between engaging in participatory democracy for the common good and for private profit becomes clear.

We can summarize engagement thusly: add a feedback loop or strengthen an existing one which has been allowed to wither or decay.

2. Transparency. As I have described above, transparency is anathema to crony capitalism and the State Elites, for the truly profitable looting, embezzlement, profiteering, price-fixing, State-mandated monopolies, public pension gaming, etc. can only occur in secrecy or purposeful obscurity. I have also noted that it is the nature of capitalism to establish cartels, oligarchy and monopoly as the most profitable alternatives to competition, and to cloak or mask these structures behind facades of free-market capitalism.

The State also has a tropism for secrecy, as all the partnering of the Elites and the State gives the lie to the separation of powers, free-market capitalism, and all the rest of the intellectual framework which supports the status quo.

On a household level, transparency can take the form of an accurate household budget. Without this transparency, then prudent planning is impossible. This holds true for households, enterprises, towns and nations.

The primary goal of an engaged citizenry is thus public transparency in service of this question: *cui bono*--to whose benefit?

Transparency might be called "the three Ts" because it implicitly requires Truth (as opposed to facsimiles of transparency, misrepresentations, deceptive accounting, manipulated data, etc.) and Trust that the feedback from auditors and oversight mechanisms has not been compromised by Elite and/or State interference/influence.

Without truth and trust then transparency degrades into just another simulacrum of authenticity packaged for propaganda purposes.

3. Accountability. A key goal of propaganda, simulacra, facsimiles, misrepresentations, manipulated data, disinformation, secrecy and complexity itself is to misdirect or diffuse accountability from those benefiting from looting, embezzlement, bribes, fraud, sweetheart contracts, gaming the system, monopoly, etc.

There are two ways to eliminate accountability: break the link between action and consequence--that is, incompetence or criminal behavior draw no countering action such as termination, investigation, clawback of embezzled funds, etc.--and confuse/craze the chain of responsibility so that no one individual or group of individuals is held accountable for their actions (or inaction).

For individuals and households, accountability starts at home.

4. An Adult Understanding (Triage and Trade-offs). As we have described above, the marketing/media complex and entitlement/victimhood mindset propagated by the Savior State have both encouraged and incentivized a *permanent adolescence* which is dominated by avoidance of accountability, justifications, excuses, instant gratification, self-destructiveness, low competence, profound internal insecurity and a reliance on shrill claims of victimhood and need.

Engagement, transparency and accountability are incompatible with permanent adolescence and require what I term *an adult understanding* of life: that cost-benefit analyses are required on all time scales (short, medium and long-term) and that trade-offs must be made in all situations. An adult understanding grasps the necessity for triage, the always difficult and occasionally ruthless sorting of dead-end strategies from those which may yet be productive. Distinguishing needs from wants is also a form of triage.

As the Savior State implodes in insolvency, permanent adolescence will yield ever more marginal returns (the greater the effort and energy invested, the lower the returns). Recognizing that is the first step to an adult understanding.

A productive second step is seeking to leverage existing assets (financial, skillsets, networks, etc.) and reworking incentives to reward productivity, creation of value and surplus.

5. Redundancy/Distributed Risk/Hedging. One of the key tenets of this entire analysis is the rising vulnerabilities and risks created by long, fragile supply chains and highly concentrated wealth, power and production. Examples abound: if all the electrical power to a region is carried by one set of transmission lines, then that system is far more vulnerable to disruption than one with multiple or redundant lines.

This is yet another case in which markets fail at the least opportune time. It is more profitable to concentrate production and transport than to distribute over a network, and much cheaper to rely on one line or center of production than to invest in redundant systems. Thus when the sole supplier/transport fails or is disrupted, the market spirals into panic because there is no short-term alternative source or supply.

At the household level, hedging, redundancy and distributing risk comes down to actions such as: having a backup skill, trade or alternative source of income; when wheat is cheap, then buy quantities in secure storage against the inevitable time when it become dear; when gasoline is cheap, buy a futures contract which will rise in value if gasoline skyrockets in cost.

Put another way, distributing risk lowers the vulnerability of an entire system. In the present era, the rentier-financial Elites and the State have colluded on a breathtakingly profitable simulacrum of distributing risk.

Ignoring the real world of depleted soil, crumbling aqueducts, aging power lines and extremely vulnerable global supply chains of essential commodities, the State/Elite sought to limit risk by financial legerdemain alone. Thus real-world risks were mitigated by essentially intangible derivatives contracts.

Rather than invest in costly real-world redundancies like power transmission lines, alternative production facilities, etc., the Elite put capital to work in credit-default swaps, futures and other derivative contracts to offset real-world risks.

In terms of profit potential and risk-return--the metrics of free-market capitalism--these State-enabled financial instruments were immensely more profitable investments than investing in actual tangible systems.

In other words: don't grow more grain, simply leverage financial bets such that profits flow from "risk management" rather than production of tangible goods. But if grain is in severely short supply, then a handsome profit in derivatives won't feed the citizenry.

This is the end-state of the Power Elite's financial *windfall exploitation*: intangible wealth and tangible scarcity.

For households, distributing risk means hedging against shortages and high costs of essentials, and developing redundancies and alternative sources of income and essentials. The goal is to preserve purchasing power of current assets, which means tracking the relative value of commodities, precious metals, currencies and tangible goods.

A key tool in maintaining purchasing power and capital is *relative strength* or *relative performance*: that is, comparing the shifting values of different assets classes to identify peaks and valleys. By buying during the valleys and selling at the peaks, we can maintain purchasing power and perhaps even grow our capital.

One way to illustrate this is to price a house in loaves of bread: how many loaves of bread does it take to buy a house? Removing the dollar (which is relentlessly depreciated by the State via inflation) from the equation offers insight into the real value of both bread and housing.

This is why many investment professionals look at the ratio of gold to oil to identify the valleys and peaks in those two commodities. When gold buys a large number of barrels of oil then they sell gold and buy oil. When oil rises in relative value to historic extremes, then they sell oil and buy gold.

From this perspective, the dollar itself is not a universal measure of value but just another commodity to be compared to other commodities.

We might summarize our focus on minimizing or offsetting risk and seeking opportunities to bolster purchasing power with these two questions:

Where is the opportunity?

What is threatened?

6. Radical Self-Reliance. This is not so much an option as the only strategy with any probability of sustained success, as this analysis has revealed the inevitability of the devolution and collapse of the Savior State and its partnership with the rentier-financial Plutocracy.

This principle follows from the necessity of opting out of the current doomed system and opting into one with a future: distributed/ networked/ reciprocal self-reliance.

Put another way: radical self-reliance requires constructing a parallel economy and society which is no longer dependent on a financial Plutocracy and Savior State as these intertwined systems devolve into insolvency.

Radical self-reliance requires a distributed/hedged and thus durable system for all forms of power--political, financial and the FEW resources (food, energy, water)--and an engaged, active citizenry to limit state and Elite over-reach/dominance.

Radical self-reliance means accepting the end of the Savior State and taking personal responsibility for one's health, livelihood, education, energy, food, retirement and pursuit of happiness.

Radical self-reliance depends on self-organizing networks of mutual interest, benefit and reciprocity/exchange rather than debt-serfdom or dependence on State swag.

Radical self-reliance values production over process and recognizes energy is the ultimate form and measure of wealth.

Radical self-reliance plans in depth for contingencies, constantly updating "Plan B" alternatives and "Plan C" emergency measures.

7. Reciprocity. The Savior State rests on two pillars: the demographic accident (a large Baby Boom generation and postwar productivity) which enabled entitlements to appear sustainable for a few decades, and the dependence of both the Elites and the non-productive classes on State largesse. That is, the granting of monopolies and the enabling of looting/gaming the system and the transfer of income from the productive class to the dependent classes.

By fostering the dependence of both the Elites and the unproductive, the State has made both complicit in its dominance; those drawing welfare, corporate or underclass, are in essence colluding with the status quo in return for their share of the State-distributed largesse. The State effectively "bought" their compliance and political silence; the only chatter voiced by the dependents is shrill advocacy for ever-larger slices of State largesse.

Once the State implodes in insolvency or an utterly devalued currency (your $2,000 a month pension remains nominally intact but now only buys a loaf of bread) then dependence, collusion, complicity and noisy claims will no longer be rewarding strategies.

In the durable, stable alternative to dependency on the Savior State, the key value and strategy is as old as human nature itself: *reciprocity*. Rather than demand something based on ones' perceived needs, the rewarding strategy will be to offer something of value in exchange for some other store of value. The *offering* comes first, then the establishment of relative value, and then the exchange.

This is a complete reversal of the State/dependency relationship in which the demand came first followed by the transfer from the State. This mirrors the adolescent/parent dynamic in which the spoiled, whining child demands largesse from the parents--an unhealthy, crippling relationship.

In capitalist terms, the investment in productive services or goods comes first, then the establishment of value and then the exchange (sale) can be transacted.

In very practical terms on the household level, you bake a peach pie and share it with your neighbors/network. If it has value, then this "investment" and freely offered value launches a reciprocity of exchanged value: someone will offer to watch your children or elderly parent in exchange for a peach pie, etc.

Yes, some people will take the slice of peach pie and offer nothing tangible in return. But the transaction nonetheless created valuable information: either the recipient placed no value on the offering, or they have nothing of value to exchange, in which case they can be excluded from future offerings of reciprocity.

Those who create no value and who offer nothing freely will soon receive nothing. This too is as old as humanity. The freeloader is shunned and left to his/her own devices. The incentives to reciprocity and creating some value which can be exchanged are high indeed, and the disincentives to permanent adolescence, dependence and fraud/cheating/freeloading are equally high.

Those who are completely helpless and without family (orphans, the completely disabled, the severely mentally ill) will of course depend on the surplus and generosity of the community. Ultimately, the smaller the surplus of real value generated, the less there will be to share. Thus the focus must shift from demands for largesse to generating true surplus rather than the debt-based (and thus bogus) "prosperity" of financial legerdemain.

Once the State collapses in insolvency, the corporate dependents (Power Elites) who had arranged monopolies, collusion and various forms of fraud and embezzlement via the State will be left on their own in a newly competitive world. Those accustomed to an unproductive life subsidized by the Savior State will also discover a new world of incentives and disincentives.

Shrill demands will gain nothing; the entity which vacuumed up surplus from the productive to distribute to others will have devolved or dissolved. The new paradigm will be reciprocity based on freely offered goods and services. The only way to get anything will be to offer something of value first.

8. Diffusion of power and the means of wealth/income creation. Widely distributed ownership of the means of production and power is the foundation of a stable economy and democracy. Recall that inequality is lowest when wealth is widely diffused and highest when income and wealth are highly concentrated.

This diffusion does not require any State-mandated transfer of wealth or income; rather, all that is needed is to end the State's current redistribution of the national income and wealth to the Elites. The State enables and enforces countless cartels and monopolies which concentrate wealth, income and power in positive feedback loops which protect and extend both corporate and State monopolies.

The diffusion model calls for widespread ownership of the means of production (land, tools, innovation, factories, workshops, distribution centers, skills, energy production, etc.) and a flexible, resilient network for exchanging energy, ideas, products and services.

9. Base Decisions on an Integrated Understanding. The mass media/marketing complex (i.e., talk radio, TV "news", etc.) is conceived and manufactured to distract, confuse and misdirect "consumers" into conveniently manipulated narrow passageways: false ideologies, simplistic divisions, life reduced to shopping, integrity sacrificed for financial gain, etc., all of which distract the citizen from an integrated understanding of the State's inevitable insolvency and the collusion of the mass media with the financial Plutocracy which owns it.

An integrated understanding rests on these foundations:

A. Ask "to whose benefit?" at every step of an investigation and digging for a complete, truthful answer.

B. Ask where did this good or service originate, how and where was it manufactured, and what are its full lifecycle costs, that is, the costs not reflected in the price tag as they have been covertly transferred to the community at large. (For example, costly-to-clean sludge is dumped in the Bay for taxpayers to clean up.)

C. Be skeptical of answers provided by self-serving mass media, Power Elites and high-caste State technocrats and elected officials, all of which are beholden to the Power Elite's interests; be alert for propaganda, simulacrum and misinformation aimed at masking self-serving Elites' exploitation and dominance.

D. Subject every transaction/purchase/decision to an adult cost-benefit analysis on all time scales, seeking to reveal marginal returns, hidden costs and comparing the value offered by alternatives--including doing nothing, or saving the surplus to be invested elsewhere at a later date.

E. Investigate the consequences of participating in the transaction, purchase, contract or network; ask what else could have been done with your energy, time, capital and skills.

A practical example would be to reach an integrated understanding of food/diet and its effects on human health. One would quickly ascertain that packaged food and fast food contain unhealthy amounts of fat, sugar and salt and thus must be consumed only occasionally and in small quantities.

An integrated understanding of food and diet requires the growing of actual food to understand the process, the work, the disappointments and the joys, and to taste the difference between a agribusiness product (for instance, a tomato) and a garden-fresh tomato.

It also requires learning how to cook and an acquaintance with nutrition--that is, what the human body is selected to find nutritious and what is inherently unhealthy to humans.

Without an understanding of how food is grown, what is inside packaged and fast foods, how to prepare healthy cuisine and what effects food has on health, then one cannot claim to have an integrated understanding of food, diet and health.

Without an integrated understanding, it is essentially impossible to make responsible decisions or choose productive, positive strategies for full-spectrum prosperity.

10. Leverage capital, assets and skills. In the long view, societies, enterprises, communities and individuals fail when they pour scarce capital and labor into projects with increasingly marginal returns. Examples include constructing large stone monuments on Easter Island while you denude the island of trees and strip the surrounding waters of fish, or drilling for oil in such marginal conditions that the value of the oil extracted barely exceeds the costs of extracting and processing the oil.

In each case, the unasked question is: what else could have been done with this capital and labor? Would other investments have generated higher returns? What perverse artificial incentives are in place which reward misallocation of capital and labor?

Alternatively, societies, enterprises, communities and individuals prosper when they leverage existing capital, assets and skills in ways that multiply positive outputs. In many cases leverage leads not to increased production but radically reduced consumption, which boosts surplus even more effectively than marginally increasing output. In vernacular parlance, this can be summed up as "doing more with less."

Speaking of perverse incentives: the ability to borrow virtually unlimited sums of money encourages grossly inefficient extravagance. That in a nutshell is the crippling context of the U.S.A.

11. ESSA: eliminate, simplify, standardize and automate. Rather remarkably for such common-sense principles, these methods of leveraging capital, assets and skills are widely ignored because the State and Plutocracy have erected various perverse incentives for unrestricted borrowing and money printing, marginal returns, crony capitalism, financial fraud and State collusion with Elites.

Once borrowing is no longer unlimited and surplus must be generated, a new set of incentives takes precedence and ESSA suddenly makes sense.

12. Generate value and surplus (working capital). As noted elsewhere in this analysis, the U.S. has not generated a true surplus for decades. It has instead borrowed trillions of dollars from surplus-generating nations and relied upon an essentially fraudulent trade of paper dollars for tangible goods from abroad.

At the household level, generating surplus (capital, savings, etc.) has been replaced with borrowing and ever-rising debt--the very epitome of unsustainability and inevitable ruin.

13. Secure/produce/innovate the FEW resources (food, energy, water). I have stressed throughout this analysis the supremely misleading artificiality of an economics and economy based on metrics such as "GDP growth," "banking profits," etc. which are fundamentally disconnected from the real world we inhabit, a world in which soil, water, food and energy are of paramount importance. Financial legerdemain and metrics are rendered utterly worthless by severe shortages and degradation of the FEW resources, as no amount of paper currency can be exchanged for tangible goods when the shortage is severe.

If citizens are hungry, with no prospects for relief, then "GDP growth" is revealed as a conceptual artifice if not outright intellectual fraud.

The scale of our dependence on abundant, easily transportable cheap fossil fuels is almost unimaginable. The U.S. consumes some 19 million barrels a day of oil, and it produces about 30,000 barrels of biodiesel. Other alternative sources of energy are equally marginal. An integrated understanding (as opposed to a facile, superficial propaganda-based "understanding") of energy reveals that there are no cheap, easy abundant substitutes. Natural gas and uranium face their own limitations, and alternative energy sources are costly--until such time as the oil supply chain breaks down, at which point it will be too late to fabricate an alternative infrastructure.

Neither the market, a self-serving financial Power Elite nor the current insolvent State are likely to secure the FEW resources for the common good, for all the reasons outlined in the above analysis. The goal will have to be understood and pursued on a much smaller scale--city, town, community, enterprise, neighborhood and household.

14. Think, plan and act with integrity. Ultimately, our personal integrity is the only value and capital we control entirely. The status quo's intellectual framework which enables and encourages corruption, artifice, misrepresentation, deception, collusion, gaming the system, propaganda, simulacrum, facsimiles and exploitation depends on each of us surrendering our integrity to serve the State/Power Elite's interests, in exchange for a share of the loot.

15. Pare complexity to simplicity. While ESSA (#11) includes "simplify" as a process, the purpose is specifically efficiency and the reduction of wasted energy, labor and capital.

But complexity is not just a wild tangle of inefficiency: *Complexity is a weapon, tool and strategy of control and dominance.* As noted in a previous chapter, the most effective way to game a system (open a windfall to exploit) is to create layer upon layer of obscure complexity: pension guidelines piled up since 1935 into a thick morass only the gamers claim to understand, tax codes which run into the tens of thousands of pages, regulations so complex only a well-funded fiefdom or corporation has the resources to decode the intent and loopholes, and so on.

As noted in the full *Survival+* text:

Complexity creates *information asymmetry*--unequal access to information--and opens up vast opportunities for gaming the system. Thus complexity itself is a tool of domination by Elites and the State. Like its conceptual twin transparency, simplicity is the mortal enemy of Elites key weapons of control: secrecy, obfuscation, disinformation, information asymmetry and complexity itself.

Thus the first step in solidifying and concentrating control (and thus power) is to create a *complexity fortress* of cloaked information guarded by restricted access and specialized knowledge. Once *information asymmetry* has been institutionalized, transparency is impossible and the gaming (and thus the looting) can begin.

The status quo Elites and high-caste technocrats will defend their institutional information asymmetry and complexity fortresses like life itself because these are the ultimate defense of their privileges, power, control and wealth. The wailing, whining and protests will all boil down to this: simplicity is impossible, complexity is necessary, and so on.

This is disingenuous. The tax code of the U.S.A. could be written on one page. Such simplicity would absolutely destroy all the privileges, loopholes and windfalls the State has constructed to benefit and protect the Power Elites. This is why simplicity is the mortal enemy of power concentrations and the Elites who control the power and national income/wealth.

These fifteen principles are scale-invariant, meaning that they apply to small and large-scale enterprises equally, from households to enterprises to cities to nation-states. These principles apply to everyone, regardless of ethnicity, creed, color or class.

In the next chapters, I will sketch out how the principles can be applied to each of the three levels: household, community/ enterprise/ network and nation.

If I was asked to draw up an "action list" derived from the above principles, it would include these items.

Many people are smarter and more experienced than I am; they will figure out solutions which work for them in their situation. I don't claim to have solutions for anyone--recall that the way the "problem" is posed sets the "solution."

Regardless of the situation, these principles are at least a good place to start.

An integrated understanding is not dictatorial or coercive. It focuses our attention on what's in our best interests and attempts to avoid/limit what is self-defeating or self-destructive and thus not in our best interests.

1. Add a feedback loop. On the household level, if there is no accurate, transparent budget of true income and expenses, then assembling such information is adding a feedback loop which did not exist before. If you write an email to your city council representative, you are creating a feedback loop which did not exist before.

Magical thinking and wishful thinking have no feedback from reality, hence they too are doomed.

Making realistic assessments means obtaining feedback from reality. Engagement via AADD and/or OODA is adding feedback loops which do not exist when we sit passively by.

2. Stop watching network/cable TV except as a rare guilty pleasure. A responsible parent limits his/her children/teens' time absorbing the destructive propaganda of network/cable TV/videogames;

what works for kids works for adults, too: everyone in the household should be restricted to an hour or two of "guilt-free TV" a week. (Now that the TV propaganda has migrated to the computer via the Internet, then that also means limiting exposure to MSM propaganda on the computer.)

Setting limits forces a healthy triage: having to pick your favorite two or three shows and letting go of all the rest is a good exercise.

The way to stop being poisoned is to stop taking the poison.

As I hope I have made abundantly clear, the primary means of controlling our experience and thus manufacturing our passive acceptance of a debt-serf "Plantation" economy ruled by a partnership of the State and rentier-financial Power Elite is the mass media/marketing complex owned by a handful of global media corporations.

To stop the poisoning of our souls, spirits, minds and lives, the solution is simple: stop watching.

The "news" is not "news"--it's carefully filtered propaganda. "Talk radio" is entertainment, not engagement; it too is another form of propaganda. (Who owns the radio station networks and how much money do they reap off "talk radio"? *Cui bono*--to whose benefit?)

The only hope of avoiding pure propaganda is to read a variety of sourced materials. If you get your "news" from one source, then the editor has shaped your experience. The only way to avoid that is to become your own editor: browse a variety of sources on the Web, including independent blogs and reputable global sources such as *The Economist, Wall Street Journal, New York Times, The Atlantic, National Review*, etc. as well as smaller local publications.

Reading reports from overseas is a good way to avoid confirmation bias which is the tendency to read only what supports your current views.

As noted above, TV programming offers the attractive illusion of value: the cooking show, the travel show, the history program, etc. have some content beyond entertainment (which remains their primary goal). But the "content" is a facade of real knowledge; a hundred hours of watching cooking programs teaches less than fifteen minutes of actually cooking/baking.

In that sense, every hour of passive watching takes away an hour which could have been spent acquiring some individual capital (skills, knowledge, etc.).

Many of my blog readers report that the solution which works for their household is to cancel cable TV entirely or even get rid of the household TVs.

There are so many wonderful documentaries and films, why waste a minute on completely worthless network/cable TV programming? This is why I maintain lists of movies and documentaries (as well as books) on my website. I don't keep exact count but the lists include over 600 books and films--many suggested to me by readers.

3. Remove your money from money-center/investment banks; "starve the beast" of fees, interest and the use of your money. Place your money in credit unions or small local banks which actually recycle the money into your own community. Transfer your 401K accounts out of money-center accounts, and place your IRA funds in your own control.

Stop paying interest to the rentier-financial Elites; pay off credit cards, auto loans and even mortgages if at all possible. Make exiting debt-serfdom a goal. Pay cash or pay off your credit cards each month. Stop generating huge fees via "churning" debt (refinancing, etc.) unless you eliminate debt in the process.

4. Grow some food yourself, no matter how modest the amount. The mass media/marketing complex would have you believe this is trivial and thus "it makes no sense in dollars and cents." It also "makes no sense in dollars and sense" to have a local dairy when a corporate agribusiness dairy hundreds of miles away can supply hormone-laden milk for a "cheaper price." As I noted above, control and experiential capital have a value that cannot be measured by financial metrics.

It is not "trivial" to grow a single bean plant in a single pot on the balcony of an urban apartment or rooftop; it is vitally important because it is within your control and the experiential knowledge gained cannot be replaced by any commodity.

5. Only buy food with real ingredients and little added salt, sugar or fat. Corn flakes and shredded wheat are examples of corporate food products which contain grain and almost no added salt or fat. Better yet, buy bulk rolled oats and stop paying global corporations to package bulk grain in their brand. Avoid packaged food with copious amounts of salt, fat and sugar. The easiest way to take control of your diet, cuisine and health is to stop buying packaged food and fast food entirely and only eat real food except for an occasional guilty pleasure.

6. Consume less of everything. The marketing politics of experience is that more is always better. The exact opposite is true; less is always better. The big house is just more work to clean, more costly to heat, etc. Bigger portions means more weight added to the consumer and thus lower health/higher risks of chronic illness, etc.

7. Start valuing control. As I have described above, control is an under-appreciated asset. The reason to own something is that you then take control of it. If it is not productive then get rid of it, otherwise it ends up controlling you. Nobody makes us buy or eat specific things; taking control means breaking free of the mass-media/marketing mindset of impulsive, distracted, excuse-dependent permanent adolescence.

This is why it is critical to own your own means of production: your own tools, knowledge and network of exchange.

8. Start valuing experiential capital. The most bizarre aspect of the consumerist *politics of experience* is the way it replaces experience of real life with the act of shopping and buying. Want to express your love for someone? Buy them a gift. Want to become more fit? Buy an exercise machine or shop for a gym membership. This bizarre substitution of highly profitable simulacrum for reality is so pervasive that it has become difficult to experience anything beyond this shallow consumerist imprisonment.

This is why I invested so much of your time earlier in this book on understanding the *politics of experience* and how it is shaped and manufactured to benefit the State and Plutocracy at our expense.

9. Seek an experiential understanding of well-being. Once again- -how can we claim to understand well-being when we haven't experienced it? The simulacrum of well-being is "sold" at stupendous profits: magic pills of one sort or another, bogus "prestige" items--the list is endless.

Ask any experienced physician for the "magic formula" and the answer will be simple:

A. Lower stress (in my analysis, re-align expectations with realistic assessments of what's in your best interests: less "prestige" and more purpose)

B. Eat a healthy diet (a diverse variety of real food cooked at home, and some home-grown)

C. Be active (there is no substitute for being fit; all that's needed is six square feet of open space)

D. Realize the mind, body, emotions and spirit are one (emotional health and physical health are one; know your own limits, strengths and challenges; be a friend to yourself and others; express yourself honestly; seek a humble understanding of Spirit, etc.)

E. Be grateful rather than resentfully entitled (the baseline is always zero; no food, no electricity, no clean water, no income, no power, no friends, no family, no social order, no Internet, no citizenship, no entertainment, no health, no shelter, and so on)

All of the above become much easier once you turn off the TV, radio, videogame and computer.

10. Become an engaged citizen. If you do nothing else, vote out the incumbents. If they were doing such a great job, why is everything corrupted and falling apart?

Beyond the few minutes it takes to vote every two years, choose one issue to engage: local schools, bikeways, the local flea market/farmers market, neighborhood watch, poorly maintained public parks, community recycling, etc. An engaged citizenry is the only feedback that can counter the pervasive influence of the monied Elites, which includes public unions, government fiefdoms and the usual well-funded special interests.

If "fighting city hall" is not your cup of tea, then join a *transparent non-privileged parallel network or organization* that has self-organized to fulfill some purpose or interest which you share.

One example would be a neighborhood group that cleans up and cares for the local park. As cities lose tax revenues and get squeezed by unsustainable pension obligations, they will not have enough money to pay $100,000 in wages and benefits to have a city employee adequately care for the park. Those neighbors who want a clean, safe park for their kids, families and friends will have to self-organize to get the job done.

The cash-strapped city will probably be willing to work with the group or at least not hinder its progress. Once again, I stress that such networks exist independent of State/corporate structures and thus they operate as *parallel informal power structures*.

Avoid confrontation and unlawful activity--The State seeks "enemies" it can violently repress.

11. Focus on the FEW resources in your household and community and build your own household's capital. That includes cash, tools, the FEW resources, knowledge/skills and networks.

12. Opt out of consumerist passivity and construct a self-reliant alternative which is independent of the devolving State and financial Plutocracy. The Plutocracy rules via persuasion through the media/marketing complex which establishes a politics of experience that then dictates how we experience events. This manufactured "experience" directs our thought processes, decisions and serfdom.

The rentier-financial Power Elite controls the State and thus the State's monopoly on coercion and violence. Opting out is legal and non-confrontational: turn off the media and "starve the Beasts" by reducing consumption, debt and income. Own/control your own means of production.

13. Encourage local enterprise. This ranges from putting your voice behind cutting red-tape restrictions on new enterprises in your city/region to buying real wood furniture from a local supplier/craftsperson rather than purchasing a foreign-made particle-board facsimile of furniture which will soon break apart and be hauled to the landfill. Only a sliver of your money spent on facsimile furniture stays in your own community while all the money spent on a real wood item constructed nearby stays in your community.

Furthermore, the real wood item will last decades rather than a few months.

14. Be open to the opportunities of hybrid work. One of my "jobs" is to pick up litter in the block around our home. Nobody pays me for it but it produces value: the neighborhood is tidy. Another "job" is watering the flowers in the city right of way which we and our neighbors planted. Many people have similar "jobs" which create value and for which they receive no money. Yes, we all need some paying work as well, but hybrid work recognizes value in many kinds of labor.

The core ideas of *hybrid work* are simple.

Hybrid work is fun. A variety of work is more fun and more rewarding than repeating one task.

Work projects and collaborative tasks you choose are more satisfying than those you are coerced into doing.

Hybrid work is inherently flexible.   If you don't like a task or collaboration, seek another.

Hybrid work responds to your interests and talents and to the needs of your community.

Hybrid work celebrates creating value. If you're creating music, art, theater, food, joy or a hundred other creative enterprises then the line between "fun" and "work" fades.

Creating value—be it maintaining an overgrown trail, collecting compost, working out a "good governance" set of transparent rules for a committee, mentoring someone else, organizing a multi-event street fair, tinkering with a new practical software application or a thousand other tasks both mundane and creative—gives your life purpose.

Service to others or a community gives your life meaning.

Hybrid work is a choice in today's economy for those with low-debt, low-cost lifestyles. As formal jobs become scarce, then many will have few opportunities for fulltime employment and thus embracing the endless possibilities of hybrid work will be the healthy, fulfilling choice.

Hybrid work honors and values the mundane necessary tasks of culture: collecting the garbage, sorting out the compost, weeding the garden, keeping an eye on the kids, helping the elderly get some exercise, caring for pets, providing security, and so on. The mundane and the creative and the paid and unpaid share the same places of honor in hybrid work.

15.   Join or construct networks (*transparent non-privileged parallel structures*) that diffuse concentrations of power. In today's economy, concentrated capital is rarely locally controlled. Thus union organizing is difficult because global capital simply moves elsewhere when employees demand a larger share of the corporate income.

Nonetheless, the concept of diffusing or counteracting concentrations of power (resisting financial and political dominance by an Elite or cartel) is still valid because local government remains accessible to citizen influence and pressure, and even multinational corporate/financial institutions must obey local laws.

At the community level, an Elite might dominate the school board or other institution which controls concentrations of authority or assets:

planning department, transportation council, police oversight committee, and so on. Once the Elite becomes self-serving and no longer serves the public good, then it is our duty to unseat that Elite or attempt to diffuse its power (add a feedback loop which did not exist before).

Naturally, every Elite, no matter how small or localized, will resist any dilution of its power. Thus the strategy is to form self-organizing groups and networks which are large enough and robust enough to match the concentrated power of Elites.

Alternatively, citizens can bypass the entire established Power Elite and form alternative/parallel structures: charter schools, farmers market co-ops, and other types of *parallel informal power structures* which operate independently of status quo structures dominated by Elites.

One example of this is to simply pay off and then close credit cards and other loans owed to the banking cartel and establish local merchant credit as needed. Small contractors have accounts at the local lumberyard which they pay off monthly. This is a form of local credit that requires no global banking cartel's involvement.

A web-based self-organized local group could share local credit availability (local credit union, informally organized private lenders, etc.) which exist independent of the global banking cartel. "Starving the Beast" (that is, no longer paying the banking cartel fees and interest) is a boon to the local economy as that money circulates locally rather than being shipped to New York, Zurich or Hong Kong.

As noted before: the possibilities for self-organizing, transparent non-privileged parallel networks are virtually unlimited.

16. Work from core principles. (Add more principles as you see fit):

1. Engagement
2. Transparency (trust and truth)
3. Accountability
4. An Adult Understanding (Triage and Trade-offs)
5. Redundancy/Distributed Risk/Hedging
6. Radical Self-Reliance
7. Reciprocity
8. Diffusion of power and the means of wealth/income creation
9. Base Decisions on an Integrated Understanding
10. Leverage Existing Capital, Assets and Skills

11. ESSA: Eliminate, Simplify, Standardize and Automate

12. Generate Value and Surplus (working capital)

13. Secure/Produce/Innovate the FEW Resources (food, energy, water)

14. Think, Plan and Act with integrity

15. Pare complexity to simplicity

Applying the Principles to Communities/Enterprises

The key feature of communities and enterprises is that membership is voluntary. One can quit, move away or otherwise opt out of membership.

By "community" I mean any self-organizing group of people. That includes school districts, transportation districts, farmers markets, building co-ops, organized swap-meets, churches, local sports leagues, local small-business associations, bicycle clubs, and hundreds of other organizations which self-organize around a specific purpose or interest (*transparent non-privileged parallel structures*).

Enterprises are organized to enter and profit from a specific market. These can be sole proprietorships, corporations, community co-ops, non-profit educational centers, performing arts councils, city-owned utilities, and so on. The key feature of an enterprise (by my definition) is that it does not depend on grants from a government--grants which are essentially non-market redistributions of tax revenues directed from concentrations of power.

Thus the arts council must charge customers money for a service rendered in a market (be self-supporting) to be an enterprise.

The distinction is not arbitrary. Since the devolution and eventual insolvency of the Central State is inevitable, then any organization depending on State redistribution of tax revenues for its livelihood is doomed. A community may be called upon to support such organizations with donations of money and goods, but that requires an entirely different understanding. In essence, the group is serving a market which generates no financial activity (for instance, a homeless shelter). If the community values the service, then it will support it. If not, then the organization must seek another market or go out of business.

There is potential overlap of community and enterprise. Municipal-owned utilities are both community-based and enterprises.

Applying the Principles of Systemic Response to communities and enterprises is largely self-evident: public business should be conducted publicly (transparency), and so on. Participation and thus payments are essentially voluntary and thus there is a "market" even if there are no "customers" in a retail sense.

Feedback from users, customers and those paying the bills (such as property owners paying property taxes to support a school district) is the essential feedback loop.

Monopoly and cartel are the enemies of efficiency, opportunity, transparency and liberty. The solution is all cases is competition from new sources. If a utility is mismanaged, then customers need to opt out and be able to choose a new source. Since the State enforces the vast majority of monopolies, then the State's devolution will open up the possibility of ridding ourselves of monopolies and cartels.

If the municipal trash service is overpriced and provides poor service, then the public should have the opportunity to choose a private trash service. If the State has granted a private trash service a monopoly contract, then the monopoly must be broken.

It is important to understand the feedbacks in both local government and non-local enterprises.

A brief story will help illustrate the key role of local government in countering the concentrated power of Power Elite Capital.

A small community/town has abundant fresh-water resources. A large multinational corporation approaches the town council to purchase the rights to the water. The multi-billion dollar corporation sees the water as a windfall inviting exploitation, and so they present what appears to be a windfall to the small city leadership: new jobs, a new park, stable tax revenues, and so on.

But the small-city government is no match for a global corporation which possesses the great advantage of *information asymmetry*: the corporate leadership knows their own long-range plans while the city leaders know only what the corporate public-relations team decides to tell them.

Given the legal thickets of water rights and contractual laws, the global corporation can easily construct a *complexity fortress* that is essentially impenetrable to the inquiries of the small-town leadership.

Presented with what appears to be a windfall, the town leaders agree to the corporation's contract.

Very quickly, information asymmetry flashes its polished teeth: the company decides to renege on various employment and public improvement promises, citing "market conditions" or other excuses. The town residents soon discover that the ceding of their water rights is legally unbreakable but the promised dividends from the global corporation are all rescindable without recourse.

The corporation, of course, has a veritable army of attorneys and consultants to defend its rights, while the township has none.

While I have endlessly pointed out the inevitable implosion of State finances, this does not mean local or even national government is superfluous.

It simply means that the Savior State which has over-reached and sold itself to Power Elites will collapse.

At a fundamental level, the citizenry has feedback into the government/State. Even in despotic dictatorships, the people can arise and overwhelm the dictatorship's army or secret police. Where votes are held, depending on the level of corruption, then citizens may actually be able to eject their political leadership via the ballot box.

As poor and limited as this may be, it is still a powerful feedback loop.

With enterprises, then people have the feedback of opting in (buying the good or service) or opting out (not buying). Their decisions as "consumers" is their feedback.

But concentrated global capital can ignore local consumer feedback.

Thus the townspeople who were essentially swindled out of their town's water rights can boycott the global beverage corporation but their votes as "consumers" weigh less than a mosquito to the global multi-billion dollar corporation. In other words, despite the propaganda about "the power of consumers," consumers have essentially no feedback into global corporations unless they are organized on a vast scale.

And since self-interest discounts most small purchases (just as it discounts the innumerable small fees and taxes imposed by the State) then no large-scale body of consumers can be motivated to expend energy on behalf of a small town which ceded its water rights to a global corporation.

The global company holds all the power and all the advantages. The only entity with sufficient power to counter that of concentrated global capital is the State. But since global capital can easily purchase the cooperation of the State, then what recourse do citizens possess?

Local government is still marginally in the hands of the citizenry--if they demand it.

At least there is a feedback mechanism: votes, boycotts, protests and the like still influence elections at the local level. Demands for transparency in city council deliberations and decisions might actually be met because the local Power Elites still depend on local citizens for their power base.

Unlike the Central State and global capital, the local power Elites cannot afford to ignore the feedback from their citizenry. Local government can raise capital via special assessments and taxes. This means it can raise enough money to counter the worst excesses of information asymmetry when dealing with concentrated capital. It also means it can construct its own complexity fortresses to mask the insiders' looting and sweetheart contracts with local Power Elites.

Whether that locally raised capital is spent wisely or squandered depends on an engaged citizenry.

In other words: no local community can field the resources needed to fend off global capital without an engaged citizenry who can disempower local Elites should they sell out to concentrated capital (rentier-financial Elites). The blandishments of global capital will win the day unless the local Power Elites are effectively guaranteed of losing their own power.

The same can be said of school board members, church officers, and indeed any power Elite in any organization. Protected fiefdoms generate monopolies, cartels and other forms of looting and exploitation. An active, engaged citizenry is the only feedback that can counter the forces of windfall exploitation and concentrations of power.

As all levels of government become insolvent, then local government must be forced to leverage what remains after the insolvency.

Here are two examples of leveraging existing assets, solutions and skills.

If devolution of fossil fuels proceeds as expected, then providing safe avenues for non-auto transport might prove beneficial to a community. In the current paradigm, then costly plans will be designed by costly consultants for new bikeways, cross-country skiing trails, elevated bridged and so on. All are good ideas but once money vanishes, then as per Principle 10, the alternative is to leverage what assets and solutions already exist.

Thus a city could "create" a bikeway (and a cross-country ski-way in winter) by simply closing off an existing central street with a few concrete bollards and a few signs. The cost of this leveraged solution is extremely low, well within the means of a small community. The bollards and the signs could even be produced locally.

Yes, the closing of a street is a politically fractious issue. The benefits must outweigh the disadvantages in the eyes of the community and an open, transparent debate may or may not resolve the issue. But the point is that solutions that leverage existing capital, assets, skills and solutions need not be costly.

In the current paradigm, a town or city seeking low-cost housing faces borrowing stupendous sums of money and a raft of complex restrictions to build new "affordable housing" which ironically ends up costing a fortune.

In the model of leveraging existing capital, assets, skills and solutions, then the city inventories abandoned properties, checks which are delinquent in taxes and notifies the owners (or the last known owner) to pay up/fix up their "public nuisance" property.

If the owners do not respond within 30 days (or if ownership has been so muddied by mortgage-backed securities, foreclosures and other financial complexities that ownership is no longer unambiguous) then the city acquires the properties via eminent domain and auctions the properties off to anyone who contractually agrees to restore the property to habitability. (If they fail to do so, they forfeit the property.)

The total cost of increasing the available housing in this manner is a mere fraction of the costly "build and maintain housing" model. This approach leverages the existing assets and solutions at low cost to the community government's taxpayers.

Indeed, many cities with shrinking populations and far-flung housing are acquiring and then dismantling housing in just this fashion, as a means of shrinking their boundaries to manageable urban cores.

When money was essentially free--redistributed and/or printed by a Central State--then solutions could be costly because insiders had a windfall to exploit. Once the State largesse is gone, low-cost leveraged solutions will be seen as "idea windfalls" which can be exploited at very low cash costs.

Placing alternative solutions in the public domain via the Web before the implosion of the status quo is of paramount importance.

As detailed above, reforming the status quo is fundamentally impossible, just as its devolution and implosion are inevitable. But the process of reaching a new understanding is not instantaneous; new perspectives the solutions need to be presented and discussed long before the devolution spins into insolvency. Like seeds, they must be distributed into fertile ground before any harvest is possible.

The key understanding here is that the process of transformation requires a certain length of time--the process of anger, denial, bargaining, acceptance and hope--and the last step, hope, needs practical solutions grounded on an integrated understanding of the problems.

Since structural reform at the national level is essentially impossible for the reasons outlined earlier, then the fundamental alternative solution is to bypass or diffuse concentrations of capital and power via *transparent non-privileged parallel structures* and *parallel informal power structures*--what might be called *small-scale counter-government*.

One goal of every community should be to offer purpose to those willing to work.

As described in previous chapters, paying work will be in short supply, but unpaid work will be plentiful. People need purpose and meaningful work. The loss of purpose and meaning is as devastating as the loss of a livelihood, and the over-arching goal of every community, however small, should be to provide purpose and the opportunity to participate by leveraging existing organizations: citizens watch committees, farmers markets, building co-ops, churches and church-based groups, city parks foundations, volunteer-based animal shelters, etc., and encourage the establishment of new transparent, non-privileged organizations formed around specific interests and purposes.

Such civic groups already have an organization set up to manage volunteers; there is no need for a costly (and thus unsustainable) new bureaucracy.

The Internet is an essential "utility" for self-organizing networks and communities, transparency, reciprocity, trade and citizen engagement.

Cities and towns would be well-served by making the Internet available (via a tax or fee which explicitly and solely funds Internet access for the entire area) to all their citizens via "free" broadband wireless service and library computers. The goal should be to enfranchise every resident, even those without computers.

Compared to other services, Web access is modest in cost given its tremendous leverage. "Free" (paid for and controlled by the local community/city) is not just another example of low-cost leverage but also of the guiding goal of community: create equal opportunities for engagement and enterprise.

As a large entity, towns (or groups of nearby towns) and cities may be able to bypass the existing monopolies which control the Internet in many locales.

Internet access is one "utility" (along with the FEW resources) which cannot be ceded to distant global corporations. Local control of Internet access and FEW resources is essential.

(The benefit of local control of local resources, assets and community is that those without Internet access--hopefully few if the community provides it--can just walk into meetings and participate via the real world.)

The usual arguments in favor of the status quo--that is, State and global Power Elites' control of all key utilities, assets and sources of financial capital-- rest on variations of this financial case: "costs are lower for global corporations due to their large scale, and we will all benefit from lower costs."

True, until they're no longer low--monopolies and cartels sole reason for existence is to raise prices without losing customers--or available at any price.

As noted above, control has a value which cannot be completely reduced to financial metrics. Global capital could care less if the people in your community have Internet, food, water or energy; this is the fundamental reason why control of these resources and assets must be developed locally--even if it "costs more."

Once again the Chinese proverb encapsulates this truth exactly: *When you're thirsty, it's too late to dig a well.*

Local communities have the same Elites as everywhere else, Elites which will fight to protect their monopoly (on trash service, cable TV, education, etc.) or fiefdom, and the only way to avoid the exploitation of monopoly and fiefdom is competition in a transparent market.

This is true of all markets. Recall that profits are highest when the risks of competing have been removed via monopoly, cartels and State fiefdoms, and insider/Elite fraud, looting, gaming the system, embezzlement, price-fixing, etc., are cloaked, obscured and hidden.

Thus the two key demands of engaged citizenry should be transparency and competition in transparent markets. These are the only mechanisms which counteract Capital and Elite's tendency to gather ever greater concentrations of power.

The goal of community action--county, city, town, neighborhood-- should be to create equal opportunities for engagement and enterprise.

As the State devolves and implodes financially, then the unsustainable "rights" to healthcare, housing and other entitlements will vanish. The local government will be better served by focusing on leveraging opportunities for engagement and enterprise rather than attempting to redistribute dwindling tax revenues.

One example is providing limited Internet access (via wireless hotspots, computers in the library, etc.) to residents. Compared to healthcare, housing, etc. the cost of Internet access is modest, and could be paid for with a small local fee collected for that express purpose.

This goal can also be expressed by the old saying, *The Lord helps those who help themselves*. The goal is creating equal opportunities for engagement and enterprise, not equal entitlements. Thus a community could regain control of abandoned properties as outlined above and then lease the open parcels to residents for gardens. Unused plots would revert to the community, but those willing to work the land could build a small source of income from these community-owned, individually worked parcels.

Conventional wisdom states that wealth flows from a concentration of capital: that is, the factory in town generates the wealth that supports the residents. While large-scale enterprises should certainly be welcomed (manufacturing, biotech, research and development, etc.) as long as control of resources remains in the hands of the community, it is misleading to discount small enterprise as an engine of diffused income and wealth. To assert that a community without a large-scale enterprise is doomed to poverty is to blindly put one's faith in the "factory model" of wealth production.

As noted in previous chapters, the Scalability Trap quickly reduces the workforce of any scalable manufacturing to low levels. Thus the communities which pin all their hopes on a factory coming to town find that the factory closes a few years later and the global capital moves elsewhere to exploit some new windfall.

The wealth of the community flows from low-cost opportunities for enterprise and the widely distributed ownership of the means of production.

Rather than counting on the hopeless prospect of mythical entrepreneurs renting empty storefronts for thousands of dollars a month, cities and towns should acquire abandoned/tax delinquent commercial properties, open up a few walls and rent out small stalls within larger spaces for a nominal fee. Once the opportunity cost is low enough, people will take a chance on starting enterprises. If all it costs is $120 a year to rent a space, then the "owner" won't have to make much to turn a profit.

If energy is the ultimate source of wealth, as I assert, then local communities might decide to raise capital incrementally and build a community-owned source of electricity. Using the "kumiai" model discussed above, a community could buy a drilling rig as community property and hire local crews to drill and install geo-exchange systems to provide heating/cooling. Those who put up capital could then have a system installed on their property for a deep discount.

Community and enterprise are not mutually exclusive; they are different aspects of the same system of local, distributed ownership of resources and the means of production and the encouragement of enterprise.

The more FEW resources and enterprises which are locally owned and controlled, the more wealth and income remains in the community.

Communities would be well served by organizing a non-monetary structure of purposeful work and enterprise.

The system of formal salaried/permanent paying job will, for all the reasons stated earlier, decline. As noted earlier, people need meaningful work not just to create value and surplus capital (be it money, tradable hours of labor, energy credits, or any other store of value) but to have the meaningful life which is part of full-spectrum prosperity.

Everyone has something to contribute; even a person who is no longer mobile can be "eyes on the street." What is fading is not work that needs to be done but the notion tat someone somewhere will pay large sums of money for that work to be performed.

Given the realities outlined in previous chapters, it seems future work is very likely to be flexible in nature: that is, a person might perform a mix of paid and unpaid/bartered labor in a variety of fields rather than one "career" which is supposed to be their "life's work." Some may choose this but few will be paid formally to do the same work for 30 or 40 years.

Thus the entire formal "factory" model of production and wealth creation and paid labor is shrinking (the Scalability Trap mentioned earlier) and a new much more flexible, less autocratic structure of work and enterprise must be constructed. Such concepts can also applied in large-scale enterprises; see Maverick: The Success Story Behind the World's Most Unusual Workplace.

Thus a critical role for the community is to facilitate the growth of a parallel system of work being freely chosen and "invested" in meaningful tasks.

Preparing for this alternative to the "factory/lifelong career" paradigm of work requires a revolution in our understanding of not just work but education and training--topics I cover in the next section.

Here is one last example of how communities can create paid work and value without relying on a factory to generate jobs: consider a high-tech manufactured product like a solar panel. Those who assert only factories create wealth do not have an integrated understanding of the entire supply chain.

In terms of labor, the factory is the least part of the entire system, especially as scalability drives the costs ever lower. If we examine the costs and labor of the entire system, the manufacture of the panels is a relatively modest part. From the factory, we add shipping through various hands, delivery to a wholesaler who adds a slice of overhead, and then delivery to a resaler which assembles other components (inverters, rooftop frames, etc.) into a system which is then installed onsite.

Of the total paid labor, very little is at the factory.

Thus local communities actually have considerable leeway in capturing much of the paid labor in the entire system. Every kilowatt of power generated or saved by sustainable locally controlled productive energy assets (geothermal, solar, wind, hydroelectric, etc.) means the significant income which used to stream out of the community now stays in the community.

Recall my previous description of the "plantation economy" in which a handful of monopolies/cartels extract the wealth of the "plantation" debt-serfs. Please count the number of global owners of mass media. There are perhaps six. Global oil/natural gas distributors: perhaps six. Global manufacturers of large commercial aircraft: two. Global banks which own/control the vast majority of bank branches and consumer debt in the U.s.: perhaps six. The number of major retailers in the U.S.: once again, a mere handful accrue the vast majority of sales. Phone service: a handful. The number of global pharmaceutical companies: perhaps six.

If you add up how much of your monthly income flows to global cartels of concentrated capital, you may find that the overwhelming majority of your income flows to cartels (mortgage, credit card, auto loan, Wal-Mart/Safeway/Target, mass media/cable TV, pharmaceuticals, gasoline, etc.) and taxes paid to the over-reaching State.

This is the very definition of debt-serfdom, which is sold as a "consumer paradise." Given the stupendous rivers of money which flow out of every community in the land to concentrations of capital and control, is there any wonder why communities are impoverished? Just imagine how different it would be if all those trillions of dollars went to locally owned banks, local farmers markets, local energy sources, and so on, and if citizens were no longer debt-serfs paying most of their income to service debt of one kind or another.

A tremendous sum of money which was previously diverted to global cartels would circulate in the local community.

This is the power of looking at systems not just in the limited perspective of "consumerism" (the lowest cost must always be the "best" choice) but in terms of control, production of income and wealth and what serves the best interests of the community in the longer run.

Once again I return to the idea that global supply chains are inherently fragile and total dependence on global capital and long global supply chains for FEW resources is simply imprudent when measured in risk management terms.

Everything is "cheap" until it isn't, and then it's no longer available at any price. As for the global cartels: it's not their concern, it's ours.

Chapter Twelve: Structuring the New State

The idea that the mighty Ming Empire was vulnerable to collapse did not exist in Imperial Beijing in 1634, yet ten years later the Dynasty fell in a sudden paroxysm of disorder, conflict and shifting loyalties.

Even as the financial and moral infrastructure of the Empire crumbled around them, complacent Roman commentators were still trumpeting a line of magical thinking that somehow Rome was too great to fail. A few years later, their magical thinking failed and the Western Empire collapsed in a heap.

We stand now at a similar point. The reach of the American Empire seems undiminished and incapable of collapse. Yet beneath the superficial solidity projected by the mass media and the State, the financial and moral infrastructure of the U.S. is crumbling rapidly.

The adolescent fantasy of the Savior State--that paying $100 in taxes would yield $1,000 in benefits--is being propped up by the mad borrowing of trillions of dollars each year: a "solution" doomed to insolvency.

In essence, the feedbacks which resisted State and Plutocracy over-reach have been overwhelmed, enabling a vast extension of the State/Plutocracy partnership's share of the national income and wealth.

The mass media--a corporate cartel within the State/financial-rentier Elites--has masked this fundamental dynamic with an unprecedented campaign of mutually reinforcing propaganda and marketing.

Those trapped in the various ideological boxes cannot escape their self-made prisons. "Progressives" are abjectly terrified by the prospect that a central Savior State might implode, as they are unable to see that the Savior State's vast programs only serve to enrich the Elites while indenturing the productive and buying the complicity of the unproductive.

In another iron box, "conservatives" are incapable of understanding that the entire project of financial-rentier Elites is to subvert free markets with the State's connivance, and to establish carefully obscured "shadow" branches of governance and banking hidden behind the Elites' predatory-capitalist monopolies and State-protected cartels.

Shrill cries to "defend free market capitalism" by weakening the State's already fatally weakened regulatory structures are tailor-made to support the Elite's unopposed concentration of capital and power. Thus the "conservatives" are the most blindly vociferous supporters of the

Elites' strip-mining of the American citizenry and economy.

In a third locked box are Libertarians who place a naive faith that a passive, weak State is the "solution" to the Elite/State partnership's dominance. But they fail to understand that concentrations of global capital and power are delighted to find passive weak States, as they offer no resistance to exploitation of a multitude of windfalls. Weak, passive States are ontologically kleptocracies, as the citizenry have no feedback into either the State or the "shadow" government and financial systems of the Power Elites.

As I noted before, all the ideologies are catastrophically wrong in their understanding of the dynamic between State, markets and Power Elites. "Progressives" are convinced that free markets are rapacious and a vast central State must dominate and control the market lest it devour the citizenry.

The real dynamic is precisely the opposite: the Elites' primary drive is to subvert competition and establish the lowest risk, highest return situation which is monopoly or cartel protected by the State. Rather than protect the citizenry by throttling transparent markets, the State hands dominance to the Power Elites who have eliminated the threat of competition by partnering with the State.

For their part, "conservatives" are blind to capitalism's intrinsic drive to eliminate competition and exploit all windfalls without regard to the social and environmental consequences. Thus weakening paltry State oversight--the exact goal of the Power Elites' monopolies and cartels--does not "strengthen" competition but speeds its destruction.

No enterprise--be it a sole proprietorship, a global corporation or a national government--can spend more than it creates in surplus.

The U.S. economy has not generated a surplus in decades; the difference between what we have earned as surplus capital and what we have spent has been borrowed or paid for with fiat dollars created out of thin air.

This con is unsustainable over the long term. Just because we as a nation have continued the con for decades does not mean the con will not catch up to us at some point. Rather, the con is unraveling right now as the world grows nervous about the instabilities being created by our profligate spending and borrowing. Every level of the U.S. has embarked on an unprecedented explosion of borrowing and debt: the central State, local government, corporations, banks and consumers.

Exponentially rising credit is fundamentally a fraud. Regardless of whether you applaud or decry the Federal government's skyrocketing obligations and promises, it is guaranteed to collapse in insolvency.

History suggests there are two paths to this end-point, and obsessing over which path we will ultimately take is less important than the end-state. Either a profligate nation's currency falls to near-zero value (also called hyperinflation) or the State runs out of the ability to borrow enough money to fulfill its expanding obligations. It then defaults on its debts and other obligations.

We in the U.S. have lived like every day is Christmas for years; whatever excesses are desired, we have purchased them by creating money/credit out of thin air. More MRI machines in Western Pennsylvania than in the entire nation of Canada? Yes, it's our "right" to have as many MRI tests as we desire.

The ability to create and spend "free money" has distorted reality for so long that we as nation now consider this magical ability to save little and create no surplus and yet spend as freely as we desire as our "right."

We have repealed reality with a gigantic con--the exponential rise of credit and debt--but reality cannot be completely replaced by magical thinking forever. Thus we can foresee the financial collapse of the Federal government within the next decade (by 2021). The mighty engines of credit creation, market manipulation and propaganda are straining at maximum RPM, and they may yet create one more asset bubble which will extend the con for one more cycle.

Or they may fail to inflate yet another asset bubble, in which case the devolution will begin sooner rather than later.

It is important to note once again the ad hoc nature of the Power Elites' and the State's response to the unprecedented challenge of maintaining exponential credit expansion.

Perhaps some of the players actually believe that infantile incantations and magical thinking will enable infinite credit bubbles into the future, but it is more likely that they are reacting in ad hoc fashion, hoping that their propaganda, credit expansion and massive State giveaways of "free money" via deficit spending will stave off disaster long enough for them to contrive a sustainable Plan B.

Alas, that hope is pure fantasy. Exponential credit and deficit expansion is not sustainable.

Many observers look ahead and see a future in which the U.S.

Federal government has dissolved, and the 50 states of the Union break into small city-states or natural units of governance. Some see this as inevitable, others as preferable.

I have tried to explain that there is no "either-or" choice to the State, Elites and markets. The citizenry have no feedback into global capital except to opt out wherever possible from feeding the Beasts (cartels and oligopolies). But the citizenry do have feedback into the State-- if it has withered, it can be strengthened, or a new citizen feedback loop can be added to the governance system.

Predatory global capital has no concern for the well-being of the citizenry of any landscape, town, city, state or nation; their concern is simple: dominate markets and States sufficiently to eliminate or bypass competition, and exploit all available windfalls to the fullest. Thus slavery and its modern equivalent, serfdom in the developing world and debt-serfdom in the developed world, are the ideal (lowest-risk, highest profit) ecologies for concentrated global capital.

But predatory global capital has its own crises: as I described earlier, global capitalism is suffering from a terminal crisis of over-capacity and over-accumulation. Having exploited the low-labor costs windfall created by the opening of Communist China, global capital had to create new "debt plantations" in its home markets via asset bubbles which could be leveraged into new consumer spending.

This "financialization" of the global economy has triggered unintended consequences; the end-point of all these machinations and manipulations is global financial implosion.

Now that consumers have maximized their debt and the last global asset bubble in housing has burst, global capital has no new windfalls to exploit except rising tax revenues diverted by the State and funneled to Power Elites via government "programs." But as credit expansion fails to create new spending, then tax revenues are collapsing; global capital and State Elites are both reduced to creating money/credit out of thin air and funneling these new trillions into the State/financial Elites' coffers.

But this fraud, this giant con game, cannot long endure. Thus the citizenry will face a choice: slip into fatalistic acceptance of ruin, or form a new government from the ashes of systemic financial ruin.

The State is the only concentration of power strong enough to counter over-reach by global capital Power Elites.

Yes, the State can be co-opted and captured by Power Elites; that is the current status of the U.S., where the citizenry are passive, fractured, besotted by consumerism and distracted by ideological propaganda and theater. But an *engaged, active, well-informed citizenry* can wrest control of their State, or reconstruct it once it has imploded into financial insolvency.

The role of the State is simple: to limit the over-reach of Power Elites and deny them the non-competitive monopolies and State-enabled cartels they ceaselessly seek to impose.

The role of the citizenry is to be engaged in governance to limit the over-reach of the State and to fend off the very partnership of the State and Power Elites which we have described in this analysis.

If the citizenry slip into passive complacency, the Power Elites (which exist in all eras and all civilizations) will gladly exploit the open windfall/power vacuum and grasp the reins of the State.

I have already described how the "balance of powers" in the U.S. Constitution has failed to limit the emergence of a "shadow" system of governance and banking/finance which flourishes within the Federal State/Elite partnership. Once again: no regulatory system, even one as thoughtful as the U.S. Constitution, can operate without citizen feedback and engagement. There is no system on Earth which can be set up to counter Elite influence and then left to run on automatic.

We in the U.S. have become complacent and disengaged, and as a result our government has been co-opted and captured by the financial-rentier Power Elites, whose mass media have obscured this reality behind a "we live in a consumerist paradise" politics of experience.

As devolution takes hold, technocratic "solutions" will be presented by all the engines of Elite control: the think-tanks (conceptual lobbyists), the "liberal media" which represents the high-caste technocrats who serve the Power Elites, and various theocratic schemers hoping to exploit the vacuum left as the intellectual framework which supported the State/Elites partnership for the past 60 years is discredited.

The Power Elites' media and high-caste flag-bearers will ceaselessly tout essentially worthless "reforms" to extend the dominance of the Elite/State partnership. Rather than succumb to these blandishments, the citizenry must make the key economic decisions in their own best interests; the market and the State regulatory agencies are the two primary mechanisms of implementing democratic decision-making.

Thus the citizenry must focus on insuring the transparency and power of these two mechanisms: transparent, competitive markets and regulations which limit monopoly, cartels, price-fixing, crony-capitalism, embezzlement, fraud and the pernicious panoply of "shadow" institutions, inventory, banking and governance.

We might summarize the three sources of feedback in U.S. governance thusly:

1. Rentier-Financial Power Elite (Plutocracy): These concentrations of power are comparable to feudal fiefdoms that wield great authority over the State and enforce the loyalty of their technocrat minions.

2. Aristocracy: high-caste technocrats, policy mandarins, think-tank/State apparatchiks (the revolving door) and corporate/State cartel contractors.

3. Citizenry, divided into two populations: those with the time, interest and will to become engaged in constructing a new framework of governance and those who do not. Both could be transformed by The Remnant, as the ideas of a New State percolate and eventually influence the unengaged and powerless.

We might also consider these historical conditions of revolution:

1. A profound crisis in the status quo leadership (the Elites no longer control events)

2. Rising hardships suffered by the productive class--often a collapse of purchasing power or the equivalent, an unbearable spike in the cost of living

3. A rise in social unrest and political engagement by previously disenfranchised and unengaged citizenry.

No one can save us from ourselves except ourselves. We have enabled the capture of the government by Power Elites and passively allowed the Elites and the State to over-reach to the point of terminal instability.

When the central State defaults or implodes financially, we can devolve into hundreds of fiefdoms or establish a new American State.

It can be argued that small local governments are the ideal form of governance, but I would caution that predatory global capital would look upon the dissolution of a central State as a wonderful windfall to exploit. No small local government would be able to mount a defense of territory or financial integrity against highly concentrated capital and power.

Thus we can anticipate that while global capital will mourn the loss of its Federal fiefdoms, which enabled "one-stop shopping" for crony capitalism, the emergence of small centers of governance will provide little barrier to the re-establishment of their dominance.

The advantages of a small, limited but active New American State accountable to its citizenry outweigh the risks of central governance. The Founding Fathers decided as much and we would be foolish to dismiss the wisdom of their choice.

Our goal, then, is to establish a new model of governance to replace the failed Savior State/Plutocracy partnership when it collapses into insolvency.

The New State requires no changes in the Constitution but rather a *radical re-set* to the Constitution. Though the Constitution does not limit concentrations of power or Elite/financial domination, it also does not limit the citizen's control of Elites, should they choose to do so.

The fundamental premise of the U.S. Constitution is simple:

It is not the government which gives limited rights to the citizenry, but the citizenry which gives limited rights to the government to protect the public trust and the citizenry's rights to life, liberty, and the pursuit of happiness.

The principles guiding the establishment of the New American State are the same which guide households and communities/local government; as noted before, the principles are scale-invariant and can be applied to organizations of any size, in any era.

We might summarize the goals thusly:

1. Transparent, limited in scope and mandate; eschew global Empire.

2. Protective of its citizenry (and the public trust) rather than its Elites.

3. Cost-benefit based, i.e. only deploys its resources in extremely high-leverage (leveraging existing assets, solutions and skills) situations.

4. Regulatory goals: limit concentrations of financial and political power, enforce transparent markets, limit "shadow" restrictions on equal opportunity rather than attempting to enforce equality, and expose "shadow" political and financial structures that benefit the privileged few to the detriment of the public trust and citizenry.

5. Issue a tangible-asset based currency, forbid leveraged fractional lending and State expansion of credit (i.e. institute and maintain sound money).

6. Foster/defend/secure the FEW resources (food, energy, water) for its citizenry.

7. Limit transfer of wealth to Elites via the State and perverse incentives to misallocation of capital and the transfer of private risk to the taxpayers.

8. Encourage and enable diffused-ownership enterprise. Eliminate taxes on earned income, i.e. enterprise; the primary source of tax revenue is a simple low-percentage tax on all financial transactions (loans, mortgages, sales/trading of stocks, bonds, derivatives, sales of real property, goods and services, etc.).

Weak, corrupt central states are soon taken over by Elites and devolve into kleptocracies. Loose confederations of small city-states devolve into fiefdoms in perpetual conflict weakened by shifting alliances and betrayals; they lose the economies of scale and the potential for widespread good governance.

The goal should be a re-set to a small central State with strong institutions capable of leveraging its powers to accomplish limited goals with limited funds.

The goals should be narrowly mandated, as per the Constitution: defense of the borders and national interests (which is not the same as global Empire), regulation of commerce and banking, issuing a sound-money currency, and the establishment of common-sense, transparent, accountable good governance.

The basic rules are simple: demand transparency, accountability and enable citizen oversight and engagement. At the risk of boring you, here are the principles of good governance:

We as a nation need to construct a new understanding of government and governance, one which has not been poisoned by the current politics of experience.

Thus the tax code should be one page long: "A 2% fee will be levied and paid to the U.S. Treasury on all financial exchanges, sales and trades of real estate, financial instruments, real goods and services, without exception. No other taxes will be levied, though government agencies may levy modest fees for services provided."

This sort of radical simplicity is impossible in the current system, yet it not inherently impossible or even difficult. In proposing it and discussing it, we sow the intellectual seeds for an eventual integrated understanding of the perverse incentives of the current system and its corruption by Elites (special interests) and fiefdoms (in the case of taxes: corporations, the super-wealthy, accountants, tax attorneys, etc.)

We must be ready to establish the New State, not with a set of canned "answers" (which smacks of the usual reliance on ideology rather than practicality) but with an engagement of ideas which will form the framework for a new integrated understanding of limited yet strong governance which protects the citizenry and public trust from exploitation by Elites.

It is not difficult to start with the common ground of the U.S. Constitution and the fundamental rights set down by the Declaration of Independence: life, liberty and the pursuit of happiness.

I cannot predict nor would I dare try to predict the outcome of the coming insolvency of the Savior State. But it is my hope that the citizens of the United States of America do not retreat into fatalism or wallow in complacency, but instead grasp the nettle of self-governance and liberty as laid down by the nation's Founding Fathers.

Charles Hugh Smith, citizen and taxpayer
January, 2010

*If you are interested in the full 396-page text of **Survival+: Structuring Prosperity for Yourself and the Nation**, please go to my website www.oftwominds.com to order a copy. I have reproduced the Table of Contents of the full text below.*

The Table of Contents of the full Survival+ book:

Key Concepts from Survival+:

Plutocracy (rentier-financial Power Elite)
Integrated understanding
Windfall exploitation
Over-reach
Simulacrum (synonyms: sham, facsimile)
Full spectrum prosperity
self-organizing networks
high-caste, upper-caste (technocrat/government class)
when belief in the system fades
profound political disunity
adult understanding
permanent adolescence
Plantation-like structures
Debt-serfs
Derealize/derealization
Neoliberal Capitalist Democracy (dominant ideology)
Profound political disunity
When belief in the system fades
The Remnant
Radical self-reliance
Politics of experience
Power densities
Cognitive traps and Emotional attractors
Splendid Isolation
Stable impoverishment/ Voluntary Poverty
Internecine Conflict between Protected Fiefdoms
Quantification trap
Infrastructure of Self
Full spectrum defense of the Status Quo
Decontextualize (scale, history)
Parallel Shadow Structures of Privilege
Transparent non-privileged parallel structures
Asymmetric stakes in the game
Hybrid work
Information asymmetry
Independently constructed sense of self